The Reluctant Communist

The publisher gratefully acknowledges the generous contribution to this book provided by the Asian Studies Endowment Fund of the University of California Press Foundation.

The Reluctant Communist

My Desertion, Court-Martial, and
Forty-Year Imprisonment in North Korea

Charles Robert Jenkins

with Jim Frederick

UNIVERSITY OF CALIFORNIA PRESS
Berkeley   Los Angeles   London

University of California Press, one of the most distinguished
university presses in the United States, enriches lives around the
world by advancing scholarship in the humanities, social sciences,
and natural sciences. Its activities are supported by the UC Press
Foundation and by philanthropic contributions from individuals
and institutions. For more information, visit www.ucpress.edu.

University of California Press
Berkeley and Los Angeles, California

University of California Press, Ltd.
London, England

Library of Congress Cataloging-in-Publication Data
Jenkins, Charles Robert, 1940–
    The reluctant communist: my desertion, court-martial, and
forty-year imprisonment in North Korea.
        p. cm.
    "Japanese edition, To Tell the Truth (Kokuhaku, or Confes-
sion), was published by Kadokawa Shoten"—ECIP Dataview.
    ISBN 978-0-520-25333-9 (cloth : alk. paper)
    1. Jenkins, Charles Robert, 1940–   2. Korean War, 1950–1953—
Personal narratives, American.   3. Korean War, 1950–1953—
Desertions—United States.   4. Military deserters—United
States—Biography.   5. Americans—Korea (North)—Biogra-
phy.   6. Defectors—Korea (North)—Biography.   7. Korea
(North)—Social life and customs.   I. Frederick, Jim, 1971–   II.
Title
    DS921.6.J44 2008
    355.1'334—dc22

                                        2007033315

Manufactured in the United States of America

17   16   15   14   13   12   11   10   09   08

10   9   8   7   6   5   4   3   2   1

This book is printed on Natures Book, which contains 50% post-
consumer waste and meets the minimum requirements of
ANSI/NISO Z39.48–1992 (R 1997) (*Permanence of Paper*).

For my mother

Contents

Foreword

My first thought, I remember clearly, was: "This can't be happening." Once I registered that it was *indeed* happening, my second thought was simple: "I'm toast." It was the morning of September 2, 2004, and, as I did every morning, I was checking the major news sites that covered Japan for any new developments (this being Japan, overnight news was usually an earthquake) or features our competitors had posted since yesterday. I clicked over to the *Far Eastern Economic Review (FEER)* website, and there it was: "Exclusive Interview: Four Decades in North Korea. On a cold night in 1965, Sgt. Charles Robert Jenkins disappeared from a patrol in South Korea. Forty years later he has resurfaced. In his first interview since leaving North Korea, he tells the *Review* his story."

I read it again. And again, making sure it said what I thought it said. It did. This headline was followed by what must have been a three-thousand-word story that included, indeed, live, recent quotes from Jenkins. There was even a photograph of him sitting on his bed in the Tokyo hospital room where he had been holed up for the last several weeks.

This was, for me, a disaster. I had been on the job as *Time Magazine*'s Tokyo bureau chief since October 2002, and since the day I showed up, Jenkins was the biggest but most elusive story in the country. Just a few weeks before I arrived in Japan, Prime Minister Junichiro Koizumi made his first-ever trip to Pyongyang to meet with North Korean dictator Kim Jong-il. During that meeting, Kim made a surprising admission. True to Japan's long-held suspicions, North Korea, Kim admitted, had systematically kidnapped Japanese citizens throughout the last few decades and forced them to teach Japanese language and customs at the country's spy schools. Kim, to everyone's further astonishment, even apologized, saying he did not approve of the program and had already punished the overzealous functionaries who spearheaded it. Negotiations to normalize relations between the two countries would almost immediately break down (and remain broken to this day) over just how many abductees there were and what has become of them, but at the time, Kim claimed that his country stole only thirteen Japanese total, of whom five were still living. Two male Japanese abductees were married to two female abductees. And the remaining woman, Hitomi Soga, was married to an American. His name: Charles Robert Jenkins.

Naturally, the story was a sensation throughout Japan. And naturally the Japanese press focused on the fate of their abducted compatriots, while the Western press gravitated toward covering Jenkins, one of the oddest and most arcane icons of the cold war. Jenkins was one of only a handful of U.S. servicemen believed to have crossed the Demilitarized Zone that split the Korean peninsula in two and to have willingly defected to communist North Korea in the 1960s. For years, the Americans' fate was the subject of intense speculation, but eventually interest in them cooled. Over the decades that followed, a piece of propaganda featuring one or several of them would occasionally surface, a rumored sighting by a stray diplomat or a North Korean defector to the South would be reported, or a magazine would try to reconstruct one of their biographies by tracking down their publicity-shy families in the States. Were they unrepentant traitors, pampered wards of this odd Stalinist hereditary dictatorship? Or were they prisoners, suffering the same deprivations that almost every other resident of this brutal regime did? No one knew. And by the late 1990s, it seemed as if no one ever would. After nearly four decades, most of the four or five U.S. soldiers that crossed into North Korea were thought to be dead. By 2002, they were all drifting quickly into the realm of cold war legend—until Kim Jong-il himself yanked one of them back into the spotlight.

Within a few weeks of Koizumi's first trip to Pyongyang, North Korea and Japan had arranged a two-week visit to Japan for the five abductees that, to no one's surprise, became permanent. Either with or without North Korea's advance consent, it became clear the moment the abductees set foot in Japan that the Japanese government would never send them back. But giant diplomatic hurdles remained. First, Japan needed to get the eight family members of the five abductees (including Jenkins and his two daughters) left behind in North Korea back to Japan as soon as possible. Second, Japan wanted a full accounting of the eight abductees that North Korea claims are already dead, as well as more information on three additional citizens Japan officially believes North Korea stole. (Although some unofficial estimates have put the number of abductees as high as in the dozens, North Korea has made it clear that it now considers the matter closed and no more information will be forthcoming.) And third, the Japanese wanted to accomplish all this while remaining a key participant in the ongoing Six-Party Talks (which also included North Korea, South Korea, the United States, China, and Russia) aimed at curbing North Korea's nuclear weapons program. Despite its efforts, the Japanese government has never been able to get other Six-Party countries, even the United States, to include the abductee issue in the nuclear talks to the extent that it would like.

All of this diplomacy took a long time. Indeed, five years later, only the first objective can be considered complete—and how that happened with respect to Jenkins forms a large part of what this book is about. Koizumi did not return to Pyongyang to pick up the abductees' families until May 2004, twenty months after his first trip. In the interval, of course, the Japanese media and foreign correspondents (myself included) found plenty of other subjects to cover—Koizumi's dazzling dominance of national politics, the country's steady economic recovery, and the increasing tensions with a newly ascendant China.

But with Koizumi's surprise second visit to Pyongyang, Jenkins and the abductees returned to the front pages. After a hectic one-day trip, Koizumi returned with only the five children of the other four abductees. Despite his best efforts, he could not convince Jenkins and his two daughters to board the plane with him. Although Koizumi said he would do his best to ensure that Jenkins and his wife could live together in Japan in peace, he could not guarantee that the soldier would not be prosecuted by the U.S. government for desertion, aiding the enemy, and other military crimes. Throughout the community of people in Tokyo who follow such things, there were (accurate) rumors that the Japanese government was lobbying the United States to pardon Jenkins, while the U.S. government was adamant that no deal could be struck. Jenkins had to face justice.

By early July, the Japanese and North Korean governments arranged a meeting between Soga, Jenkins, and their daughters in Jakarta (chosen because it was, in the opinion of the family, a neutral country where Soga couldn't be taken back to North Korea and Jenkins couldn't be apprehended by the U.S. military). While the family was in Jakarta, I met with a senior U.S. embassy official in Tokyo about a different story, but as we were wrapping up, I asked him what he thought was going to happen to Jenkins.

"Well," he said, "Jenkins is a very sick man. He had an operation in North Korea just before he left, and it has gone very wrong. He needs top-notch medical care as soon as possible. So you know, I wouldn't be surprised if he just happened to show up in a hospital around here some time soon." "And then what?" I asked. "Well, we don't know just yet. We would allow him to get better, for starters. I don't think it would be good publicity to send the Marines into a hospital just to throw a sick old sergeant into the brig after forty years. Not that we'd be allowed to anyway, given that it'd be a Japanese hospital on Japanese soil. We will just have to see how this plays out. But the U.S. government is firm that he's a wanted man who must face trial."

By the end of that week, true to my embassy source's prediction, Jenkins and his family got on a plane headed for Tokyo. Landing in the early evening, under full police escort, they drove straight from the airport to the Tokyo Women's Medical University

Hospital in Shinjuku. The interest in the Jenkins-Soga family was now at its highest point yet. But there was no access, no information, and no news. The Japanese government wasn't talking, nor was Washington, the U.S. embassy in Tokyo, or U.S. Army–Japan headquarters. Repeated calls to all of them over several weeks had amounted to nothing. There were armed Tokyo police outside the hospital and, according to Japanese news reports, right outside Jenkins's hospital room door. The way many of my sources within the U.S. embassy were talking, it was pretty clear that even they didn't know much about what was going on or how it all was going to end.

Colleagues and I in the foreign press corps consoled ourselves by telling each other that the story was being so well guarded that there was no way to get anywhere close to it. On the strength of such group certainty, I authoritatively assured my bosses in Hong Kong and New York that there was nothing more that could be done. One of them told me that that was fine, if I said so, but also wanted me to know that Norm Pearlstine himself, the editor in chief of all Time Inc. publications, was personally intrigued by the story. I remember throwing up my hands when I received this information, just as I distinctly remember laughing out loud at an email from another editor in New York asking, innocently, about the likelihood of getting an interview. What a rube! How hopelessly naive! Jenkins was locked down tight, and that was that.

Which brings us back to September 2 and my career flashing before my eyes as I clicked around *FEER*'s website. Just a couple of days earlier, I had blithely assured my boss that while I wasn't making much progress, no one else was either. There was no way, I declared, Jenkins was talking to anyone. And now here he was.

Maybe this isn't real, I told myself. Or maybe this isn't as big a deal as I think it is. A quick Google News search of Jenkins's name dispelled that notion. Hundreds of hits came pouring back. It didn't matter if the *FEER* story was any good. The Associated Press, Reuters, and Agence France-Presse were all picking up the basics—Mysterious U.S. defector to North Korea speaks after forty years!—and spinning it out to news sites across the web. Within an hour or two that morning, it was the top story everywhere.

It was time to face the wrath. I picked up the phone and called my boss in Hong Kong. "Hi, Mike. Uh, have you seen the news today?" I said. "I sure have," he responded, with an iciness I had never heard from him before. He always expected the best from his correspondents, for us to break big stories like this first and move them forward the furthest, but he was also realistic about how competitive this field is and how skilled our rivals are. You were expected to win far more than you lost, but it was also understood that it is impossible to win them all. So on those occasions when I felt like I had gotten beaten on a story, I could usually expect a pep talk from him, not a chewing out. Today, there would be no pep talk. Indeed, there was very little talk at all. Since after a few moments, it seemed he was too mad, disappointed, or upset to actually speak to me, there wasn't a whole lot to say. "So, um, yeah, I'm going to find out how this happened," I said. "I suggest you do," he responded, just as icily, and hung up.

The author of the article was named Jeremy Kirk. At least by byline, I knew just about everyone who covered Japan for a major Western publication, but I had never heard of Jeremy Kirk before. Turning back to Google, I entered his name and hit "Return." From the hits, it was clear he worked for the *Stars and*

Stripes in Seoul. Reading his stories, it took only a couple of minutes to figure out that he spent a lot of time on the courts-martial beat, and many of his stories quoted defense counsel Capt. James D. Culp who—dammit, dammit, dammit—had been assigned as Jenkins's lawyer only a couple of weeks ago. So obvious. Culp was the way to get to Jenkins.

Actually, it had always been obvious that Jenkins's defense lawyer would, at this stage, have better access to the man than anyone else. But knowing what I knew about military lawyers, both on the defense and the prosecution side, it never occurred to me that one might make his client available for an interview. While civilian lawyers were generally well-versed in the benefits and pitfalls of engaging the press, military lawyers still seemed more beholden to the military culture of press silence. A military lawyer who wanted press exposure for his client was a concept so alien, I never considered it for longer than it took me to dismiss it. Clearly, I had misjudged this military defense lawyer.

"Michiko!" I called out to the office next door, where sat one of the three Japanese reporters *Time* employed along with me in the bureau. "Yes?" she said, as she popped her head around the door. "Can you find out where Jenkins's lawyer, a guy by the name of Capt. Jim Culp, is staying? Call every hotel if you need to, but he's staying somewhere in Tokyo. It's important." Less than three minutes later, she returned, saying she had found him. "How did you do that so quickly? Where is he?" I asked. She said that anyone in the U.S. Army staying in Tokyo was almost certainly at the New Sanno, so she called the front desk, asked for his room, and hung up after they put the call through. Again, so obvious. Of course he was at the New Sanno, a luxury hotel in the heart of Tokyo that is owned and operated by the U.S. military and restricted for its exclusive use.

I sat down and banged out a rather desperate letter to Culp saying I had read the *FEER* article with intense interest but that *Time* would be a far better venue if he really wanted to get Jenkins's story out there. I carried it over to the Sanno's front desk that afternoon.

A few days later, I got a phone call. "This is Capt. Jim Culp," the voice said. "I got your letter. We should talk. Come to the New Sanno at 7:00 P.M. tonight." I arrived at 7:00 sharp, and he was waiting for me outside. As I approached, I called his mobile phone to confirm that I had the right person. He was a big guy. About my height, 6'4", but thicker through the shoulders and chest. Balding, probably mid-thirties. Scowling. Definitely playing the hard guy. He was not going to make this particularly easy. We exchanged greetings, walked into the lobby, and, as discreetly as he could in such a public place, he turned me around and patted me down here and there, across the back and across the chest, under the arms, on the pants pockets, he said, to make sure that I wasn't wearing a wire. "This whole conversation is off the record, you understand?" I said I did. "In fact, until further notice, I will deny that this conversation ever took place, you understand?" Again, I said I did. "OK," he said. "Let's get some chow." (I have gotten his permission to recount our conversation here.) Rather than heading outside and into Tokyo like I expected, he turned around and headed for the Embarcadero, the New Sanno's sports bar.

The Embarcadero, I am almost ashamed to admit, is one of my favorite places in Tokyo. While I love almost everything about Tokyo, homesickness is an occasional hazard of the job.

And while there are tons of American-style bars all over Tokyo, they all seem to have admittedly small yet significant lapses in authenticity (such as ketchup that is too sweet, club sandwiches that come with chopped egg in them, or Budweiser signs but no actual Budweiser). The Embarcadero, however, is authenticity itself. Great burgers, absolutely mammoth martinis, American beers on tap, nonstop American sports on TV—and you can pay for the dirt-cheap bill in dollars. Since even Americans need a military host to get them in, however, I would, over the years, routinely ask my military sources to take me here. But now, being here with Culp, I felt a little strange.

"What are we doing here?" I asked as we sat down in a back booth. "Considering you just patted me down for a wire, it seems like you're worried about being watched or listened to, so why are we staying in the middle of a military hotel?"

"No," he responded. "I was worried that you would tape our conversation or write a story about it, and that would be bad for my guy. I take it as a given that everything I do and everything I say is being watched by the CIA and military intelligence. Wouldn't you? God, for the good of the country, I kind of hope that they are. I mean, if you were in the CIA, don't you think I would be a can't-miss surveillance target? The lawyer of an accused defector to North Korea who they think might be a communist spy? Um, duh. I assume everything I do is being watched, so all I have to do is make sure I don't do anything illegal or unethical. And the only reason I am here and talking to you is because I think it may be in the best interest of my guy, which is my first priority and legal duty. So start talking: Why do you want to meet him?"

Despite our mutual wariness, we got on well pretty quickly. At that dinner, we laid the groundwork for what was going to become a fruitful relationship. The hard guy act quickly melted away. Culp mentioned he had been an infantry sergeant himself years ago before he put himself through college and law school, so he could understand and identify with what his enlisted clients were going through in a way that a lot of his current peers couldn't. (That was part of the reason, I assumed, that Culp always referred to the man he represented not as the somewhat distant "my client" but as the much more intimate "my guy.") He obviously had a lot of sympathy for Jenkins. In his assessment, Charlie, as Culp called him, was a poor, dumb, unlucky soul who had done an incredibly rash, stupid, and bad thing but who had already paid beyond measure for his crime. He described him as a frail and broken man, one who had no communist sympathies whatsoever, who had suffered constant mental torture while in North Korea, and who would be lucky if he could just live out his last few years on the planet in peace and freedom.

These would all be opinions I would more or less come to agree with after getting to know Jenkins, but at the time, every word was new territory for me. It was quickly becoming clear that the *FEER* article had barely touched what was a rich and varied tale. Jenkins was still a cipher, a total unknown. Besides the other American deserters in North Korea, Culp was the only Westerner who had spent any significant time with Jenkins in the last forty years. So every word Culp spoke was a revelation.

The situation was so politically sensitive it was essential that no one make a misstep, Culp explained. The Japanese government would love the United States to just pardon Jenkins, he said, "but that ain't gonna happen." The United States had never wavered from its insistence that justice must be served. "Charlie's situation is precarious," Culp continued. "So far, Charlie has benefited from the goodwill extended to him by the Japanese people. Since his wife is a national hero, they are inclined to think the best of her husband, at least in the absence of any further info. And the United States had, at least initially, sent signals that Charlie could recuperate in the hospital unmolested."

"But that was, what, six or seven weeks ago?" Culp said. "I could see the tide was beginning to change. The Japanese press was beginning to ask, 'How long is this guy going to hang out in the hospital at taxpayers' expense?' And I could feel that the prosecution and the rest of the U.S. government were getting more and more impatient. I told Charlie a little while ago, 'I can feel it. Something is happening. They are coming for you soon, if we don't make the next move first.' And I knew I needed to take the initiative on the PR front."

"But why *FEER*?" I asked. "It is such a small magazine compared to *Time,* the *New York Times,* or any of the other publications that would have killed for that interview." "For this story," Culp said, "it didn't matter how big the publication was. *FEER* was perfect for my purposes. Our audience was not the whole world. That day will come. But this time around, the audience was actually just a few people in the U.S. and Japanese governments, to tell them to back off, to give us just a little more time and my guy will voluntarily turn himself in very soon. I picked Jeremy because, frankly, I don't know a lot of journalists, and once I decided I needed to do this, I needed it done quickly and I knew I could control what he wrote. I snuck him in and out of the hospital; they talked for maybe an hour. He had connections at *FEER*, so *FEER* it was. The story was a way of delivering a message to people I can't talk to directly, to tell them that there is no need to make Charlie's coming under custody ugly if they can wait just a little while longer. And I can feel that the pressure on him has lessened because of it. So on every front, the story was a home run, a huge, huge win for us. But next time when Charlie talks, and there will be a next time, he will want a more global audience, and maybe then it will be for *Time*." When Culp said that, toward the end of our dinner, I knew the next big Jenkins story just might be mine. (And when Culp and Kirk had a falling out several weeks later, that cemented it.) We finished the night with two double Crown Royals (Culp's favorite whiskey) and a promise to keep the conversation going.

Charles Robert Jenkins is, quite simply, a figure of lasting historical importance. He has lived a life that's unique in twentieth-century history. No other Westerner has survived so long in the world's least known, least visited, and least understood country on the planet and been able to return to tell the tale. And what he has to say is vitally important: Is there any country in the world harder to get a handle on than North Korea? And while there are certainly rivals when it comes to the intensity of American diplomatic bungling, has any country been a U.S. foreign relations debacle so consistently for so many years? While native North Korean defectors and escapees from its gulags have made some horrors of that nation known to the world, Jenkins is the first Westerner able to provide a long-term, detailed view of this secretive and brutal society from the perspective of an outsider who became intimately familiar with its inner workings. I do not profess to know much about North Korea, but I'm confident Charles Robert Jenkins knows more about it than just about any foreigner on the planet.

Perhaps this does not sound like as great a feat as it is. Very few people know much at all about North Korea, even the people who most prominently hold themselves out as experts. If from within, the nation is a prison nearly impossible to escape from, from without, it is a vault of information nearly impossible to crack into. Very few Western countries have diplomatic presences in Pyongyang. Entry for Western journalists is severely limited (I have never been), and once there, writers (like all visitors and virtually all residents) are accompanied or watched wherever they go. For this reason, because so little new information about North Korea ever leaks out, many of the stories that make their way into print are recycled over and over again for years. Throughout the 1990s, for example, it was an oft-printed truism that the U.S. government suspected North Korea possessed one or two nuclear weapons. The "one or two" total had been bandied about so long, journalists didn't even bother to source it. It was simply accepted as fact. In his book *North Korea: Another Country,* Bruce Cumings tracks the ultimate source of the story down to a 1993 *National Intelligence Estimate.* It was arrived at, he writes, "by gathering all the government experts on North Korea together and asking for a show of hands as to how many thought the North has made atomic bombs. A bit over half raised their hands."

So what about North Korea is known? To begin with, it's abundantly clear that the current, unhappy state of the Korean peninsula was born in the waning days of World War II. As victory over Japan became imminent, U.S. military planners were already looking to contain what they perceived as the next likely threat: the Soviet Union. Working to construct a power-sharing agreement for the soon-to-be liberated Korea, or so the story goes, a young colonel by the name of Dean Rusk (who would later be secretary of state under Presidents Kennedy and Johnson) arbitrarily chose the 38th parallel as the dividing point between the Soviet-controlled North and the U.S.-controlled South for no reason other than it bisected the landmass into two roughly equal halves.

Unable to settle on a common form of government, the Soviets and Americans installed regimes of their own choosing. The Soviets selected a young, former anti-Japanese revolutionary named Kim Il-sung, while the staunchly anticommunist Syngman Rhee took over in Seoul. After American and Soviet troops withdrew from the peninsula in 1949, each Korean leader aimed to unify the country under his government. Peaceful unification plans broke down. Tensions increased. After a swift military buildup and the blessing of Stalin, Kim invaded the South on June 25, 1950, to quick and devastating effect, almost conquering the entire peninsula in days. To Kim's surprise, however, the United States rose to action immediately. It rallied the United Nations, and by October, UN forces had recaptured all of South Korea, taken Pyongyang, and were headed for the Yalu River, the border between China and Korea. The push greatly alarmed Mao, and he ordered 270,000 "volunteers" into battle to push back the U.S.-led UN forces across the 38th parallel and back into southern territory. Inconclusive battles and lengthy peace negotiations continued for two more years until a ceasefire was declared on July 27, 1953. More than three million people were dead, and the borders fell almost exactly where they stood before the fighting started.

With the balance of power thus definitively laid down, Kim Il-sung went on to create one of the most idiosyncratic regimes in modern history. The cornerstone of his communist dictatorship was the concept of Juche, or self-reliance, in all things, from economics and politics to international relations and defense. He embarked upon a series of Soviet-style five-year plans that emphasized state-controlled agriculture and heavy industry as well as titanic defense spending. Simultaneously, he built a cult of personality that outdid Stalin's, one that rivals most religions in terms of fervent devotion. He fashioned himself the Great Leader: textbooks and state-controlled media invested him with almost magical powers, and towns and cities are littered with innumerable heroic murals and statues. Interaction and free exchange with the outside world was severely limited in favor of state-controlled propaganda, every citizen to this day must wear a red enameled pin of Kim's face, and his birthplace is both a pilgrimage and shrine.

While in the early years, North Korea's economy actually outperformed the South's, the inefficiencies of command economics soon appeared and, over time, intensified. Always more dependent on the communist bloc than Juche rhetoric ever admitted, North Korea's eventual estrangement from both the Soviet Union and China accelerated the country's economic decline. (Since Kim's death, the Soviet Union's disintegration and China's barely disguised embrace of capitalism—including its normalization of relations with South Korea—have hurt even worse.) Meanwhile, Kim Il-sung created one of the most militarized societies the world has ever known. One million of the nation's twenty-three million citizens are active-duty military, seven million are in the reserves, and an estimated 30 percent of the government budget goes to defense spending. A final and key ingredient of North Korea's peculiar political stew: heaping measures of anti-Americanism.

Among the central targets (both literally and figuratively) of North Korean anti-Americanism are the twenty-nine thousand

U.S. troops who still defend the southern side of the DMZ and, in cooperation with the South Korean military, the rest of the country. Since arriving in September 1945, American troops have rarely been absent from this area, and despite recent force reductions, there is little chance that America will leave completely any time soon. "Demilitarized Zone" is a misnomer, of course. The two-and-a-half-mile-wide DMZ is actually one of the most heavily fortified and militarized borders on the planet. And, until the Afghanistan and Iraq Wars, Korea was well-known as the most dangerous, least desirable assignment in the U.S. Army.

This was Jenkins's posting in the months before his decision to defect, on the front lines of the taut tripwire that separated Seoul from an uneasy peace and "a sea of fire," as one of North Korea's favorite turns of propaganda phrasing puts it. Both before and after Jenkins crossed over, that wire was frequently almost tripped. Although he played no active role in any of them, Jenkins's life was affected by all of the major standoffs the United States and North Korea had since 1964, including the 1968 capture of the U.S.S. *Pueblo* spy ship and the 1976 Panmunjom Incident, when North Korean soldiers hacked two U.S. Army officers to death over a dispute about whether to cut down a poplar tree that was interfering with U.S. sight lines in the DMZ.

Upon Kim Il-sung's death in 1994, he was elevated to Eternal President. His son, Kim Jong-il, took over as the nation's supreme (earthbound) leader. Although Kim Jong-il had been the expected successor since the mid-1980s (and had, in fact, been running much of the day-to-day affairs of the country for years), leaders in Washington and throughout the world greeted his ascension with fear and suspicion. Whereas Kim Il-sung had earned grudging respect as a canny operator and formidable foreign relations com-batant (and had the added credibility of being an actual former soldier), Kim the younger was seen as a spoiled playboy and prat, a fat and pretentious dilettante who was undisciplined and possi-bly crazy. The (poorly sourced) stories of his love for French co-gnac, fresh sushi, and a never-ending supply of nubile women, all while his people starved, were legion. A dozen years later, how-ever, those assessments of the man who in North Korea has long been called the Dear Leader have had to be revised. He has far out-lived the early predictions of his ouster or the collapse of his nation. Indeed, Kim the younger has managed to not only retain but also increase his hold on power. And he has arguably managed to con-found the United States even more successfully than his father by relentlessly taunting Washington about his country's on-again, off-again nuclear power and weapons development projects. One in-strument Kim has used to retain power is to yoke himself more tightly to the military, pursuing a "military first" policy for food and resources distribution.

Kim's successful consolidation and refinement of his powers are even more surprising considering he has managed to do so while his country's economic situation has become ever more dire. North Korea suffered two years of record-breaking floods in 1995 and 1996, followed by a summer of drought and famine during which, according to some estimates, two million people died. According to the (South Korean) Bank of Korea, North Korea's GDP has fallen from $21.3 billion in 1994 to $12.6 billion in 1998. In decades past, North Korea had been a grain exporter, but in 2001, it grew only 3.5 million tons, well below its self-sufficiency threshold. More than fifty years of disastrous Juche self-reliance has turned North Korea into one of the world's biggest food aid recipients.

When compared to the South, the North's decline is particularly striking. As late as 1965, North Korea's economy was actually three times the size of the South's. But beginning in the 1980s, South Korea's investment in international trade began to pay off and then multiply. Today, its economy has vaulted to $1.8 trillion, the eleventh largest in the world, and that country's citizens now enjoy a per capita annual income of $24,000. Once the seat of dictatorships nearly as brutal as the one above the 38th parallel, South Korea has, over the past twenty years, developed strong and growing democratic institutions and traditions, hosted an Olympics, co-hosted a World Cup, and is home to world-class manufacturers like Samsung and LG. On January 1, 2007, South Korean diplomat Ban Ki-moon became secretary general of the United Nations.

I interviewed Jenkins for the first time on November 27, 2004, just hours after he finished serving a month in the brig for desertion and aiding the enemy. With the help of Culp and another friend in the army who signed me on to base, I was waiting for Jenkins when he arrived at the small enlisted family home where his wife and daughters had been living during his imprisonment. Though Jenkins was expecting me and wanted to talk, the interview did not start well, primarily because I could barely understand a thing he was saying. Granted, he had just come off of some of the most traumatic times of his life (which is saying something, given his trauma-filled life), but as we began to speak (he did not even bother to take off his dress green uniform), I did not, at first, think he was all there mentally. Culp had briefed me about what Robert's life was like in North Korea, but I don't think it is possible to be totally prepared for one's first meeting with Robert. Chain smoking cigarettes, since he wasn't allowed any in the brig, Robert started talking about the wives of his friends (it wasn't immediately obvious he was talking about the other American defectors), women who were Romanian, Thai, and Lebanese, and all their children, who had names like Gabi and Nahi. He spoke about "the farm," "the college," and "the apartment" as if I would know what those places were. It took me several minutes to figure out that "Pin-yong," was how he pronounced "Pyongyang," and not a different town. Sometimes, forgetting who he was talking to or searching for the right word, he would start to speak Korean for sentences at a time before he realized what he was doing. Throw all of this under the thick cover of a deep southern drawl and frequent periods of shoulder-shaking sobbing, and none of it made any sense. "This is all going to come apart," I thought. "After all this, I am going to leave here with nothing."

But slowly, over about four hours, Robert and I turned things around. He responded patiently to requests to back up, say it again, slow down, explain this part, tell me the significance of that part. Thanks to that patience, I pieced together what I thought was a coherent narrative of his tale and, particularly, his plausible fear that "the Organization" (as I quickly learned he called the all-in-one combination of the Korean Workers' Party and the government) wanted to turn his Asian American daughters into spies.

That first interview served as the foundation of a five-page *Time Magazine* story that ran the next week. Already, that first day we talked, he mentioned the book he wanted to write. He said one of the Japanese foreign ministry people who helped him get from Jakarta to the Tokyo hospital had given him the idea. Before either he or the Japanese government realized that the

U.S. Army would provide a free defense counsel, the Japanese bureaucrat suggested that writing a book would be one way to pay for a lawyer.

I stayed in touch with Jenkins after the story came out, and after the media furor died down, I followed up on his book idea. "If you really want to do that," I said, "I would be happy to write it with you." He agreed, we found a Japanese publisher, and I took two months off work in the summer of 2005 to move near his home on the tiny Japanese island of Sado. Every morning, five days a week, I would pedal three or four miles on my bike from my small waterfront rental to his house. I would interview him for eight hours straight, except when we broke for lunch, eating the food that Hitomi left us before she went to work at City Hall in the morning. I would then write most of the weekend. I have tried to retain in print the very simple and plain-spoken way he has of speaking.

Those two months interviewing Robert were some of the most remarkable times of my life. It would be obvious at this point to say that there is no one in the world like him and knowing him is a consistently dumbfounding experience. He is, in many regards, a living, breathing Rip Van Winkle. As he is quick to point out, he did get some of the biggest world news over the years. He knew that a man had walked on the moon, he knew the space shuttle blew up, and, since the United States was always national enemy number one, he always had a pretty good idea who the president was. But the gaps in cultural knowledge were frequently strange. He arrived back in Japan not knowing what a Big Mac or *Sixty Minutes* was. When Capt. Culp first asked him which publication he'd like to tell his story to, he didn't say *Time* but *Life,* a magazine that suspended weekly publication in 1972.

When I arrived in Sado, I brought, as a small gift, a DVD of a movie I thought he'd like: *Bonnie and Clyde.* He had never heard of it. When he sings karaoke, he sticks to Elvis Presley songs, since they are just about the only ones in a standard karaoke repertoire he is familiar with.

As this memoir shows, some Western popular culture did slip through North Korea's media blackout, but these limited doses have had an odd effect on him. Ever since a smuggled videotape of a 1980s Michael Jackson concert somehow made its way to him in the 1990s, for example, he's been something of a Jackson fan. It always amused me that whatever was making the bulk of the entertainment headlines at the time in 2004 and 2005—whether Jennifer Lopez, *The Sopranos,* or the latest Spider-Man movie— Robert would be oblivious. But whenever a TV segment or newspaper story about Michael Jackson appeared (and this being the mid-2000s, it was always a story about his legal troubles), Robert would be sure to stop and watch or read it. "He does seem to be a lot weirder these days," Robert once said to me after watching a CNN segment about some court appearance Jackson was involved in.

As we started to get down to work, I have to admit I felt some disappointment when I determined how, generally, the arc of his life and his time in North Korea was going to go. Before I began, I had two equal and opposite storytelling fantasies. On the one hand, I thought it would be ideal if he had lived a life of decadent privilege at the right hand of Kim Jong-il, if he had acted as a kind of senior advisor or even court jester in the Dear Leader's inner circle. I would think less of him as a person, but what a great story that would have been. Or, I thought, it would have been just as compelling if Jenkins were forced to live a completely opposite life—if, for forty years, he had had to withstand the unending misery of prison, torture, and starvation. From a humanitarian point of view, of course, I would be sorry for any suffering he may have gone through, but if he had endured forty years starring in his own, real-life *Deer Hunter,* he would have been a true American hero, regardless of his original crimes.

In fact, Robert's life was neither of these. His was a life of quiet desperation, of suffering an almost unbearably understated evil. He and his fellow Americans were considered special by the Organization—about that, there can be no doubt. They led lives significantly richer in material comforts than most North Koreans were able to. But it is also clear that the North Koreans never figured out what to do with these trophies, how best to put them to use. It's another, admittedly perverse way in which much of the potential of Jenkins's life was squandered, not just by himself but also by his overlords. They didn't know what to do with him, so they let him do, effectively, nothing. Occasionally, I would ask him what he did between the years of, say, 1986 and 1990, and sometimes he would say exactly that. "Nothing. During that time I did nothing."

Nothing, except to try to stay alive and sane in a country that's effectively a giant prison. The curtain Robert draws back on the mundane, relentless, dehumanizing operation of the North Korean state—its wastes of money and labor on domestic spying rather than economic output, its language-debasing double-speak, its interference in the most intimate details of its residents' lives—helps demonstrate how insidious and debilitating, bizarre and oppressive the country is. The story of Robert's life was more difficult to tell since it did not reach either extreme of the sensationalism spectrum. He is neither a villain nor a hero, just a man trying to cope with the guilt of a horrible mistake while eking out an existence in a country unimaginably strange and hostile. But I hope that this attention to the quotidian, this focus on the struggle of everyday life, has produced a more nuanced and valuable contribution to our understanding of North Korea.

What are some of my most prominent impressions of Robert, as I got to know him? First and foremost, he is a deeply saddened individual. One story I wrote about him for *Time* was entitled "The Long Mistake," and I think that sums up well how he has had to come to terms with his life. Short of teenagers who dive into shallow pools of water, break their necks, and become paralyzed for life or drunk drivers who survive when their victims do not, I can't think of too many people who have had to live so long with an error they couldn't undo, and I can't imagine how that presses on someone's soul.

Another clear conviction: Robert tells the truth. There have been numerous times when Robert told me something that either sounded insane, trumped up, or nonsensical only to have my doubts shattered by the realization that he was—despite my suspicions or my frequently patronizing conclusion that, oh, he's just gotten a little ahead of himself—absolutely correct. As we were working on the book, some of the back stories he gave me on how the Americans' wives got to North Korea sounded a little farfetched. But, to use the most publicly vetted example, consider how almost everything he said about Larry Allen Abshier's wife, Anocha, has turned out true. When Jenkins was finally allowed to leave North Korea in 2004, he says, North Korean officials went through all of his photos (some of which appear in this book) and confiscated any that included non–family members. But they missed a snapshot with a South Asian–looking woman in the far left of the frame, a woman Robert identified as Anocha. When CBS News ran a story online about whether Anocha might be the first confirmable non-Japanese North Korean abductee along with this photo in late 2005, the story winded back to Thailand, and Anocha's brother came forward to identify her and corroborate virtually everything Robert said about her history.

That revelation proved a huge boost to Robert's international credibility and started the hunt for more non-Japanese citizens abducted by North Korea, of whom Robert says there are many. It is a topic that newspapers throughout South Asia are taking very seriously. I doubt they will have much luck in getting the North Koreans to admit anything, considering how long it took the Japanese to make headway on the issue, but it's a start. After the book was published in Japan, the mother of Jerry Wayne Parrish's wife, Siham, also resurfaced, confirming Robert's version of her story as well. After numerous similar occurrences, I am inclined to take what he says about, for example, the identity of Seoul City Sue, whether fellow American James Dresnok habitually beat him to a pulp, and a host of other topics as truthful until proven otherwise. Although Dresnok recently denied to a documentary film crew in North Korea that he ever beat up Robert in anything more than a single fair fist fight, it seems to me such an odd thing to fabricate, and a thing that reflects poorly on Robert (what soldier would want to admit he couldn't defend himself against another?), I can't imagine why he would make a story like that up.

What else? I am impressed by Robert's resilience, his tenacity, and his absolute refusal to quit. I am impressed by his desire to try to set things right, which I think comes from somewhere deep in his soul, and his willingness, at the first realistic chance he got, to risk, for all he knew, a life in a U.S. military prison so his daughters could have a better life. He's a completely ordinary man who almost literally stumbled into history yet made amends for his heartbreaking, colossally tragic error with bravery and integrity.

Jim Frederick
October 2007

Acknowledgments

I would like to thank the following people for all of their help and support:

- My wife, Hitomi, and my daughters, Mika and Brinda
- My family back in the United States, especially my mother, Pattie, my sisters Pat and Brenda, and my brothers-in-law Lee and Reggie
- The people and the government of Japan, especially former prime minister Junichiro Koizumi, Kyoko Nakayama, Akitaka Saiki, and Takashi Okada
- The people and government of Sado Island, especially Mayor Koichiro Takano and Keigo Honma (also known as Kakuhonsan), as well as Toshiaki Wakabayashi, Tatsuya Ando, Mayumi Oda, Katsue Hamada
- The administration and officers of the Niigata Prefecture Police Department

- Yoichiro and Midori Doumae, who have been kind enough to host Brinda and Mika while they go to school in Niigata
- James D. Culp
- Maj. Gen. Elbert N. Perkins, commanding general of Camp Zama
- All the soldiers, officers, staff, and their families at Camp Zama, especially those who were at Headquarters and Headquarters Company in late 2004, including Maj. Dave Watson, 1st Sgt. Eugene Moses, Sgt. 1st class Andrew Rogerson, Capt. Valerie Manuel, Japan Self-Defense Forces Sgt. 1st Class Masuhiro Ogata and everybody who worked with me in the orderly room; Maj. Steven Smyth and his wife, Emily; Lt. Col. Jack Amberg; and Toma Rusk
- Former U.S. ambassador to Japan Howard Baker and the U.S. embassy staff, especially translator Yoko Yamamoto
- The U.S. Army, the people, and the government of the United States of America
- The doctors, nurses, and staff of the Tokyo Women's Medical University Hospital
- Satoshi Gunji and Tetsuya Sugahara of Kadokawa Shoten, Hamish Macaskill and Junzo Sawa of the English Agency, and Neeti Madan of Sterling Lord Literistic
- Reed Malcolm, Kate Warne, and Jimmée Greco of the University of California Press

Prelude

When Japanese prime minister Junichiro Koizumi came to North Korea for his first, big, one-day summit with Kim Jong-il on September 17, 2002, we didn't know about it until he had already left. My wife, Hitomi, and I were watching TV that night and the announcer on the state-run news program (the only kind of news available in North Korea) said that Koizumi had been to Pyongyang for a visit, and that "repatriating Japanese who were living in North Korea" was one of their topics of discussion. The news made it sound like the two leaders talked about the fates of families with Japanese roots who, for various political and diplomatic reasons, had been stuck in North Korea since the chaotic aftermaths of World War II or the Korean War.

The show didn't include anything about the Japanese citizens, possibly numbering in the dozens, that North Korea had kidnapped from Japanese soil in the 1970s and 1980s and forced to teach at its spy schools. The show did not even mention the word "abductee," but I turned to Hitomi and said, "This has got something to do with you." She waved me off, saying, "No way."

I ran into the closet and pried up some of the floorboards under which I hid my radio. It was a little portable job that a friend of mine bought years ago from some Syrian medical students who were studying at the No. 11 Hospital in downtown Pyongyang. I couldn't get NHK (Japan's public TV and radio broadcaster) right away, but I did get Voice of America. The lead story: Koizumi confronts Kim over abductees at historic summit. I said, "God damn! I knew it!" Hitomi's English isn't so great, so I gave her one side of the earphones and translated the newscast as it was broadcast. We were stunned. Kim confirmed for the first time that North Korea had systematically stolen Japanese people for decades, and he revealed that some of these abductees, including my wife, were still alive in North Korea.

The Japanese government and media were totally surprised that someone named Hitomi Soga was one of the abducted that North Korea admitted to having still. She was not on the roster of suspected abductees that the Japanese government had submitted ahead of the meeting, and you could hear the newscasters that night scramble for details on this unknown woman. "Who is she? Where did she come from? Why didn't the Japanese know about her before? We will bring you details as we uncover them."

By the afternoon of the next day, the radio networks had started to piece it all together, and by the time I tuned into NHK that evening, they had almost the whole story. They knew not just the details of Hitomi's abduction in 1978 from her hometown on Sado Island, but that she was now married to me, Sgt. Charles Robert Jenkins, a mysterious American who, for reasons unknown, was thought to have walked across the DMZ and into the communist dictatorship on a cold January morning in 1965.

As we finished listening to the news that second night, we didn't know what it all meant or what was going to happen to us, but we did know that some people from the Organization would be coming for us soon.

And the next morning, they did.

1 | **Super Jenkins**

My first memories are of World War II. One day, late in the summer I was five years old, the fire engine in our town was running up and down the main street with its lights flashing and sirens blaring. Rich Square, North Carolina, where I was born, was a small, poor town, so the main drag was only a few blocks long and had only a single stoplight. But when the engine got to the end of the street it would turn around and come back the other way, clanging and making a racket, over and over again. I asked my mother why the fire truck was doing that, and she said it was celebrating because the war was over.

The winter before that, I remember my mother would go to a little shed in a cotton patch on the edge of town in the middle of the night a couple of times a week. She was part of a rotation with others from town pulling watch for the German air raids that everybody feared but that never came. I spent many nights in that little shack there with her, playing with whatever little wooden or tin toy I brought, while she scanned the skies.

My father never pulled air-raid watch. He was too busy working. He worked down at the ice plant only a couple hundred yards from my house, and he was working all the time. For days at a time, I would rarely see him. He was the foreman, though the plant was small. Usually he oversaw two other men at a time. He often said that the plant never took a break, so neither could he. He would come in to the house at, say, 4:00 A.M. and get two or three hours of sleep. Then he would head back to the plant, work until 9:00 or 10:00 P.M., come home and have dinner, get a few more hours sleep, and then head back out to the plant before dawn. That was typical. My father was drafted into World War II, but he never served. The doctor from our town wrote the draft board to get him out of going, not for any medical reason but because, the doctor wrote, "the town's gotta have ice."

My father was a big man, not like me. At a different plant he worked at in a nearby town called Rocky Mount we moved to for a few years, there was an elevator that would carry the five-hundred-pound blocks of ice up to the freight train cars for loading, but it broke a lot. When it did, my father would grab the blocks one by one with a giant set of tongs and drag them up a ramp to the train all by himself. At times like these it seemed like there was nothing he couldn't do.

Drinking was his weakness. He liked his alcohol, and Three Bears Whiskey was his favorite drink. When he wasn't drunk, he was all right, but drinking got him into trouble a lot. His name was Clifton Rose Jenkins, but he hated his middle name—and he was none too fond of his first name, either, to be honest. One day, one of the black men who worked for him came into the office and said, "Hiya, Clifton." This was a time when open racism was still a regular part of American life, especially in the South.

We called blacks "negroes" or even "niggers" back then and didn't think twice about it. Blacks were forced to use different water fountains and different bathrooms, and when they came to a white person's house, they had to use the back door. And when a black man talked to any white man, especially his boss, like this one was doing, he was supposed to address his boss formally— as in "Mr. Jenkins"—not use his first name. So my father, who was drunk at the time, picked a pistol out of the desk drawer and fired it at the man, missing him by only a couple of inches. A few days later, Mr. Boomer, who owned the ice plant, came down to the plant to see my father and give him hell for what he'd done. Even though it was a Sunday morning when Mr. Boomer came by, my father was drunk again, and you could hear them fighting from halfway down the street. Things got so heated that my father said, "to hell with it," and climbed the electrical pole outside the plant. Usually you need spikes to climb a pole, but my father scampered up it like a big old bear, pulled the switch, and cut all the electricity to the plant. "Let your damn ice melt!" my father yelled. Mr. Boomer later told my mother that my father was the best worker he had ever seen, but he could hardly bear all the bad behavior that came with him.

My mother was born in North Carolina, in a town not far from Rich Square. Her family, the Coggins family, were cotton farmers and so was my father's, so my mother and father knew each other when they were little kids. My father was about five or ten years older than my mother. The story goes that the first time he saw my mother, she was a baby, sitting in her bassinet. He was just a little kid, obviously, but he declared, "I'm gonna marry her some day." And sure enough, he did. My mother was a teenage bride, no more than sixteen or seventeen, and soon after they got married in 1930 or 1931, they started having kids. We had a large family. After losing twins at birth, my mother gave birth to three girls within just a few years of each other: Olivia, Anne, and Faye. Then came me, my sister Audrey, my brother Gene, and my sister Pat, who was born in 1950.

I got along with my brother and sisters well enough, and my mom always tried to make sure we had enough to eat, but that was tough. With seven mouths to feed, my parents were just barely getting by. Even in a poor town in a poor part of the country, we were still pointed at and whispered about as a poor family. At school, lunch cost twenty cents, but the poorest kids didn't have to pay. My brother, sisters, and I never had to pay. All of us wore hand-me-down clothes, whether they were church charity giveaways or from neighbors just taking pity on us. It was hard on our pride, of course, but we had no choice. The house I lived in for most of my childhood was a dump. Originally built as a warehouse, its walls were thin wood and provided very little insulation. My father split the place up into rooms. We didn't have an indoor bathroom or running water until the laws changed, making those things a requirement in every home, and my father had to put plumbing in.

There was no doubt that my father was a hard worker—one time he got a gold medal for making the most ice in the entire chain of ice factories that owned his plant—but the ice business wound up killing him. One day, a large ammonia pipe at the Rocky Mount plant broke. Ammonia was part of the process—how you made ice—because it has good properties for refrigeration, but it is also highly toxic. The pipes would break a lot, and on this day he was in one of the boiler rooms, a small place, fixing that busted ammonia pipe all day and into the night. He must have inhaled tons of the stuff. He came home late that night, maybe 11:00 P.M. or midnight. I had just turned eleven years old and was already in bed, but he came into the kitchen, took his seat at the kitchen table, and put his head down to rest. My mother turned around to the counter to fix him a plate of supper. When she came back with his food, he was dead. He had an insurance policy of $1,000, which left my mother enough money to give him a decent funeral and burial and not much else.

With her husband dead, my mother moved us all back to Rich Square, and she went to work as a nurse for a chiropractor in town. She would head to work in the morning when we went to school, and then come back around 5:00 or 6:00 to make sure we all had something for dinner. She tried to make sure we always had some meat, and I remember when we had enough spare butter to spread right onto our bread, that was a good day.

I was a troublemaker, and my mother was a strict disciplinarian. All through my childhood, I would just give her fits by acting up in school and running around town. Her favorite punishment was to sit me in a chair and not let me move or speak until she said I could go. She would leave me there for hours. When I was fourteen or fifteen, I started smoking. One time, I absentmindedly pulled a pack of out my shirt or jacket and—I wasn't even thinking about where I was—started to light a cigarette inside the house. My mother popped me in the face so fast it wasn't even funny.

I am sorry for all I put her through, but I never once doubted that my mother loved me as much as a mother possibly could. I don't know if it was because I was the oldest son, or if one of the signs of being a good mother is that you convince each of your children individually that he or she is the favorite one, but she always made me feel like I was special. For example, at school they would sell ice cream cones for a nickel during recess; money was always tight in my family, but, whenever she could, my mother would slide me an extra nickel so I could get an ice cream cone.

A few years after my father died, my mother married Dan Casper, a divorced man who drove a truck for the state penitentiary in a nearby town. He had divorced his first wife after he found her in bed with another man. He was a good enough man and treated my mom well, so we had no problems with him, though the family's finances never improved and we always scraped to survive. When I was fifteen, they had a daughter, whom they named Brenda, bringing the family total to eight children. I always felt a special closeness to my littlest sister. Since I was her big brother, she thought I was the greatest thing. When my second-youngest sister, Pat, was born, I was ten or eleven, so the last thing I wanted to be doing was holding and cuddling a baby. But by the time Brenda came around, I had changed my thinking. When I would come home, Brenda would see me and scream and climb into my lap. It broke my heart every time.

School and I never got along well. I did not like it, and I wasn't particularly good at it. I was always very good at a lot of stuff that they didn't teach in school—working on engines, doing carpentry and electrical work, and fixing things—but numbers and letters just never came easily to me. And even though I was a small guy, I was unusually strong and athletic for my size. One time, when I was a young teen, I picked up the transmission casing of a 1952 Ford and threw it on the back of a pickup truck all by myself—a feat that earned me my nickname, which I kept my whole time in Rich Square: Super (as in Superman). By the time I was thirteen or fourteen, I knew I would not be finishing high school, but unfortunately for me, you couldn't leave school until you were sixteen, so I suffered through as best I could.

I filled my time out of school working. I worked down at the grocery store every weekday afternoon for $7 a week, and during the summers I would mow lawns. Whenever I got an extra fifty cents in my pocket, I would head over to Scotland Neck, where there was a skating rink. If I went on a Monday night, there would always be some guys from the North Carolina National Guard who had just finished their once-a-week drills hanging out. They would show up in their uniforms, even though the rules said they were supposed to take them off when not on duty, because they knew the girls went crazy over them and the boys were impressed.

Watching those guys in uniform and hearing them talk about the stuff that they were doing made me want to try it. But I was only fifteen at the time, and you needed to be eighteen to join, or seventeen with a parent's signature. North Carolina and my family being what they were at the time, though, I didn't have a birth certificate, so my mom just signed the induction papers saying I was seventeen. Simple as that. Everybody who knew me knew I was too young—and, plus, here I was this skinny thing, swimming in my uniform—but without a birth certificate, nobody could prove I wasn't seventeen. Not that anybody really cared all that much. So soon enough, I became a member of D Company of the 119th Infantry Regiment of the North Carolina National Guard.

Every Monday night we would have two hours of drills in Scotland Neck. And two weekends a year plus two weeks per summer we would go to Fort Bragg, North Carolina, for rifle training and shooting practice. That first summer I joined up, I volunteered for two months at Fort Jackson, South Carolina, for more in-depth instruction in weapons and tactics, similar to what you would get in basic training in the regular army. That was one of the hardest things I had ever done. That whole first year was tough, in fact. The first time I ever really got screamed at by a regular army officer that first summer at Fort Jackson, I thought, This is not for me. But after I got used to it, I came to enjoy everything about it. The uniforms, the discipline, the way you could see yourself getting better at important skills. Even the sixteen-mile, full-pack road marches in ninety-five-degree heat. No matter what kind of hell they were at the time, when you were done, you felt like you had accomplished something. And I liked being one of the guys that showed up at the skating rink in uniform. I liked being oohed- and aahed-over rather than one of those doing the oohing and aahing.

In all, I spent three years in the Guard. When I wasn't doing Guard stuff, I worked at the Pope Motor Company, a Ford dealership near my house. I was in charge of the lot, keeping the new and used cars clean and in working order. I liked my job, and I liked working on cars. My car, a 1950 Ford with a 1955 V-8 T-Bird engine, was the fastest car in Northampton County. During one of the back road races we would frequently have back then, they once clocked me driving my Ford at 140 miles per hour. But even while working and messing around, I always looked forward to the next training session most of all.

One night after Monday drills, instead of going to the skating rink, we went to the pool hall. There I had my first drink. I didn't have but two beers before I was drunker than hell. I woke up the next morning with the worst headache I had ever had, and I swore I would never drink again. I didn't take another drink until I was twenty-one, on leave during my first posting in South Korea, in a club in Yokohama, Japan. I didn't know what to order. I didn't know the names of any drinks. I heard a soldier next to me ask for a Tom Collins, so I said I'd have the same.

I wasn't long in the National Guard before I made private first class, and it wasn't long after that that I made corporal. And then I went up for sergeant. But I didn't get it because the National Guard promotion review board asked me what I would do if a soldier under my command fled from battle. At summer training at Fort Jackson, they taught us if someone in combat turns and runs, you have to stop him at all costs, even if you have to shoot him. So that's what I told the promotion board: If one of my soldiers deserted, and I couldn't get him to return to battle, I would shoot him. Well, they didn't like that answer, even though that was what I had been taught. I didn't get my promotion. But I didn't care that much since I knew I wasn't going to be in the Guard much longer anyway. I was going to join the army.

2 | In the Army, and across the DMZ

In middle of 1958, I reached the end of my three-year National Guard hitch. They asked me if I wanted to extend or re-enlist, and I said, "Hell, no. I'm joining the army." In November I reported for two months of basic training at Fort Jackson, South Carolina, as an infantry soldier of B Company, Nineteenth Battalion, 1st Regiment. Since I had already been in the Guard, basic training was very easy for me. I didn't even have to do most of the drills, and I spent a lot of my time as a driver in the motor pool. Once basic was over, I shipped out to Fort Dix, New Jersey, for advanced infantry training. After two months of that, I was off on my first plane ride ever, to Fort Hood, Texas, to join the 1st Armored Division.

The 1st Armored Division was a true combat unit, known as Old Ironsides. Over the years, members had seen major action in World War II and the Korean War. But for some reason, whether bad luck or I don't know what, I was assigned to tend the shooting ranges. I did some of the carpentry to make the targets for the ranges, building the frames with two by fours and then fitting the spans with heavy fabric. And I made paste. I would make giant, forty-gallon vats of paste with flour, water, and Red Devil lye. We used the paste to stick paper targets to the fabric. Day to day, this was a fine job as far as it went, and I knew I liked the service well enough for the long term to get a tattoo on my left forearm of two crossed rifles above the words "US Army." It cost me $4 at a tattoo parlor in Killeen, Texas, not far from base.

Soon enough, however, I got frustrated and bored doing paste runs, as we called them. It wasn't my idea of real soldiering. I was hidden away in this corner after making private first class in 1959, and it didn't look like I was going to get promoted again anytime soon. I had heard that opportunity for promotion was good in South Korea, though, so when I became buddies with someone who worked in the office at Fort Hood that was in charge of reassignments and he asked me where I wanted to go, I told him. There is nothing like knowing people in the right places. Just a few days after telling that guy where I wanted to be, I got my new orders: I was deploying to South Korea. This would be my first tour there. That tour was to be trouble-free. It wasn't until my second hitch in Korea that I got myself into a world of problems.

I showed up at Camp Kaiser in South Korea in late September 1960. Camp Kaiser was under the Seventh Division, and it was the northernmost U.S. base in South Korea at the time. It wasn't the closest base we had to the Demilitarized Zone, but because the DMZ runs diagonally from the southwest to the northeast, Kaiser was the farthest north. I really liked my time there. I was a member of the 17th Infantry Regiment, led by Col. Lawrence S. Reynolds. We were known as the Buffalos, and it was what we called a straight-leg infantry group, meaning there was no armor or transport attached to us. "If you ain't walking, you ain't getting there" is what we used to say. It was a tight unit, and you really had to be on the ball to get along out there. We would do drills, go out on patrols, take classes, and do field problems. Standard soldiering, really. But the rumors about good promotion opportunities in Korea turned out to be true. One of the rewards for doing well at inspection was getting to be the colonel's personal guard for a day. I did this a couple of days in a row right off the bat, so I started to get to know the colonel pretty quickly. I would bullshit him a lot, to tell you the truth. I would say to him, "The men are all pulling for you to make general, sir," and "Everybody says you run the best unit in Korea, sir." He knew I was bullshitting, but I think a part of him bought it, too, because he was always especially nice to me. In February of 1961, I was promoted to specialist fourth class, and in June of that year, I was promoted to sergeant. After being private first class for so long, to make sergeant in less than a year—I have to admit, even I was surprised.

After my year hitch in South Korea and a month of home leave, I was off to Germany from New York Harbor on a boat called *Geiger Counter,* which I thought was a very strange name for a ship. I joined up with the B Company, Thirty-sixth Armored Infantry Regiment, Second Brigade, 3rd Armored Division, at Ayers Kaserne in Butzbach, Germany, not far from where Elvis Presley had been stationed in Friedberg. Here, I discovered that a lot of people resented how young I was for my rank. Many of their feelings were understandable. I was a fire team leader, which means I was in charge of half of a squad, or about five soldiers, but I really didn't know many of the basics of leading men into battle. And I don't mean the fuzzy stuff about leadership and confidence or even having what we called a "command voice"—my yelling voice has always been good—or a "command presence." I am talking about the little but important things like the rules of radio communication, since one of the big parts of leading a squad is communicating with other units. Because of the way I got promoted and how quickly it happened, I had never learned any of it. Before getting to Germany, I had never used a field radio in my life.

I'll give you an example. One of my first times out, when I didn't hear something over the radio, I would say, "Repeat." But the word "repeat" over the radio is a signal to your artillery units to fire a shell at exactly the same place they fired the last one. What you are supposed to say is, "Say again last transmission." Oh, boy, did I catch hell for that one. If I had kept doing it the way I had done it, who knows how many extra shells I could have landed on various positions. But I learned quickly and hacked it the best I could, and soon I had learned enough and gained enough respect that people mostly left me alone on that front.

I wound up staying in Germany for three years. This was a great time in my life. I was young, held a high rank for my age, and was having fun both on the job and off. When that hitch was up, I put in my top three choices for reassignment. My number one choice was South Korea, and I got it. I was excited. I had had such a good time during my first South Korean tour, I thought that nothing but good things were going to come to me there. How wrong I was.

My second tour in South Korea started out just fine. There was no indication of how horribly it would go within just a couple of months and the extreme, life-changing actions I would soon be taking. I arrived at Charlie Company, First Battalion, Eighth Cavalry Regiment, 1st Cavalry Division, in September 1964. It was a tiny place called Camp Clinch, hard up against the edge of the DMZ, north of the Imjin River and east of the treaty village of Panmunjom. It was just a handful of Quonset huts, since Charlie Company was the only unit there. The company of eighty men was so overworked and understaffed that the company commander almost danced a jig when I arrived. He called me a sight for sore eyes. Two days later, I had my own squad of twelve men. I led patrols and helped operate a lookout station that we used to keep an eye on North Korea. My station was called Guardpost Desart. The monthly schedule I followed was one week of nighttime guard post duty, one week of daytime guard post duty, one week of classes and drills, and one week of nighttime ambush patrols along the DMZ, where we would head out into the hills and lay in wait for any North Korean units with the brass to have breached the 38th parallel or any spies trying to make it to the heart of South Korea. Obviously, our patrols were designed as deterrence, and I guess this strategy worked, since we never encountered a North Korean in the short time I was there. It was a good routine, and other than the obvious tension and danger of being on the famous tripwire, I enjoyed it. For a while, anyway.

It all started going wrong within a month or two, however, when I got asked to lead what were known around camp as hunter killer teams. These were far more dangerous and aggressive daytime patrols than the routine nighttime ambush patrols. They often came under hostile fire because they were so much easier for the North Koreans to spot. While I was happy to guard the DMZ and even defend it with my life if it were attacked, these purposely provocative missions were not what I signed up for, nor did I feel they were in keeping with the unit's stated mission. But since these patrols had an air of secrecy about them, I did not know from how high up they were being ordered, which ruled out my initial idea of appealing to a higher officer to get them stopped or at least to get me out of leading them. I kept denying the increasingly insistent requests throughout November and December, but I began to panic because I was sensing that these requests to lead hunter killer teams were soon going to become an order, something, as a soldier, I could not disobey.

A week or so before Christmas, I got a call patched through to my guard post. So I got on the phone, saying, "This is Sgt. Jenkins." And he said, "Sgt. Jenkins." And I said, "Yes, this is Sgt. Jenkins." And he said, "No, this is Sgt. Jenkins." By now I knew who it was, and I said, "This is all really funny, but I am on duty. I have a job to do." It was a guy named Joseph T. Jenkins. He was a distant cousin of mine from Woodland, North Carolina, about six miles from Rich Square. Woodland was a small town with an even smaller town, called George, about a mile down the road from it. George was the home of a basket factory and a casket factory and nothing else. Whenever we went to see J. T., as we called him, we would say we were going to "Woodland, by George!" That really cracked us up at the time. Nowadays, he was a master sergeant at I Corps in an administrative unit in Uijongbu, which was about halfway between Camp Clinch and Seoul. He told me not to get upset and that he was just calling to say he was going to come and visit me in a few days.

A couple days later, just before Christmas, J. T. came to visit. He didn't stay more than a few hours, but we talked about the old neighborhoods, people we knew, girls we had dated, and girls we missed. As he was leaving, he told me that the 1st Cavalry, my division, was scheduled to go to Vietnam. In early 1965 Vietnam wasn't a war involving a lot of U.S. soldiers yet, but it looked like it was headed that way, and J. T. told me the 1st Cavalry was going to be one of the first army units to go if it came to that, probably as soon as the spring. He told me to keep it secret, but a couple of people overheard him and the rumor swept through camp. This news only added to my worry and depression. If I managed to survive the hunter killer teams, I would be faced with potentially shipping out to a new and even more dangerous war in the jungle within a few months. (I did not know it at the time, but the 1st Cavalry that wound up shipping to Vietnam was completely transformed and refitted into a helicopter unit before being redeployed, meaning that almost none of the 1st Cavalry personnel in South Korea with me went directly to Vietnam, if they went at all. Most were just reassigned to the new unit that took over jurisdiction of that area of the DMZ. I was, of course, already in North Korea by the time this happened, so I only learned about it upon my return.)

I started looking for a way out. If I got an order to lead a hunter killer team and refused, I knew I faced a court-martial on the spot. Add the additional fear of going to war in the jungle if I survived the hunter killer teams, and it seemed to me that I was doomed. I started to feel depressed and drink heavily. After weeks of private deliberation, I came up with a plan. I was cold, tired, scared, depressed, and miserable. The pain and the pressure had gotten to be too much to bear, and all I wanted was out. I know I was not thinking clearly at the time, and a lot of my decisions don't make sense now, but at the time they had a logic to them that made my actions seem almost inevitable.

Rather than turn myself in at Camp Clinch and face what I thought would be a much harsher on-the-spot court-martial, I decided that the only thing to do was go AWOL, lay low for a little while, and turn myself in back in the States. But I knew there was no way off the peninsula if I headed into South Korea—I had heard too many stories of servicemen who went AWOL getting picked up almost immediately to think that that direction could be successful. So I decided that I was going to walk north across the DMZ and into North Korea. Once there, I would ask to be handed over to the Russians and request a diplomatic exchange for passage back to the United States, where I would face charges for desertion. I had heard of this happening before. Some American soldiers in West Germany, I knew from the time I was there, had deserted to East Germany, and they got handed over to the Russians, and the Soviet Union ultimately sent them back to the States. I did not understand at the time that North Korea was not particularly close diplomatically to the Soviet Union. It certainly did not see the Soviet Union (or even China, for that matter) as its big brother and wasn't going to be handing anybody over to anyone. To us, at the time, it was all "the Communist Bloc," and we thought Moscow was the center of it, so I did not think my scheme was as crazy or unbelievable as people today sometimes seem to think it is. Obviously, it didn't turn out at all the way that I intended, but that was the plan.

In short, I went AWOL for many of the same reasons that thousands of young, desperate, misguided soldiers go AWOL every year, not because I was a communist sympathizer or because I had any affection for or intention of defecting to North Korea. I am not trying to excuse my desertion, which is a despicable crime, or the fact that I abandoned men under my command, which is absolutely one of the worst things a leader can do. But I am trying to explain that I still feel my biggest mistake was the way I went AWOL. I was so ignorant. I did not understand that the country I was seeking temporary refuge in was literally a giant, demented prison; once someone goes there, they almost never, ever get out.

I came to my final conclusion just after Christmas day 1964. The next time I pulled a nighttime patrol, I said to myself, "I am crossing the DMZ." The night I next pulled duty was about two weeks later, a dawn patrol that would begin the night of January 4, 1965, and extend into the next morning. That night, I bought two six packs of beer after dinner and went back to my quarters. I think I gave two cans away, but before patrol I drank the remaining ten myself. As I was drinking, I decided to give some of my stuff away. I scribbled a note to Sgt. Caine telling him he could have my field jacket. Then I wrote a note to a Republic of Korea Army soldier in our company, telling him he could have my gas mask. After I thought about it a little while, I wrote another note to Sgt. Caine, telling him he could have my wall locker lock also. These notes didn't refer at all to my plans, in case someone found them before I actually left. All they said was, "You can have this gas mask" or "You can have this field jacket," and I left them on their footlockers. I took a set of my best buttons, ones that never needed polishing that I had bought in Germany, from my dress uniform and gave them to another soldier. When he asked why I didn't need them anymore, I just said that my cousin at I Corps in Uijongbu had gotten me out of this place. Though I no longer remember that soldier's name, I will never forget his response: "Can your cousin get me out of here, too?"

One of the biggest mysteries of my crossing over and one I hope someone can solve someday is the issue of the letter that I supposedly wrote to my mother. Not long after I left for North Korea, I discovered after my return to the outside world in 2004, my mother received a telegram from the U.S. Army informing her that I had written a letter to her telling her the night I disappeared that I planned to leave for North Korea. I am here to say now that I never wrote the letter to my mother that the army said I did. (Many in my family never believed it anyhow. The biggest tip-off: The telegram said I signed the letter "Charles," a name I never used for myself.) Today the army says it cannot find this letter; nor can it find the notes to the soldiers in my company that I actually did write.

These days, I often wonder what the purpose of that telegram was and who ordered it sent. My own theory on how it came about is this: When I went missing, the United States had a dilemma on its hands. If I was kidnapped by the North Koreans, the U.S. Army was duty-bound to do everything it could to get me back, even if it became an international incident that threatened to turn into shooting hostilities. If I had walked, however, the United States could safely avoid the whole sticky, political issue of my rescue. But the United States didn't know which was the truth. North Korea officials could be counted on to insist that I was there voluntarily, but the United States lacked the proof to be able to either agree or contradict them. The notes I left the soldiers suggested I was walking, but they didn't quite settle the matter for good. So the army invented a note that did. The United States, of course, happened to pick the correct and, for them, safer theory about my disappearance. I did indeed walk of my own free will. But in the U.S. Army's zeal to cement the issue beyond a doubt, I believe someone, somewhere along the line, decided to fabricate some evidence.

At about 11:00 P.M., I reported for duty to my lieutenant. Either he had no idea I was drunk or decided to look the other way, because he didn't say anything. I mustered my soldiers, and we hiked about two miles toward the 38th parallel and stopped on the crest of a hill. From our position, we could clearly see Tedach-san, a mountain in North Korea. As was standard, I led my soldiers into ambush position and then radioed in my position once an hour to headquarters. We stayed hunkered down like this, miserable in the bitter cold, for about two and a half hours. It was near freezing that night. After my radioman had radioed in the second time, I told both the radioman and another soldier close to me that I was going to go ahead and check to see if the road below was clear. I told them that if the road was clear, I would start the squad back to camp.

I took out my little compass and walked slowly away from my men and the U.S. Army. Even at that time, I thought there was a chance I might turn back. I knew that I could be gone for a while, and if I lost my will, I could come back. I could say it took me longer to check out the road than I thought. Even with the notes and giving away my buttons, I knew I hadn't done anything that couldn't be undone. But about ten or fifteen minutes into my walk, I fell over a sloped ledge. It was probably fifteen or twenty feet I went sliding down. A branch tore up my face, especially my nose, something fierce on the way down, so I tried to stop the bleeding with pressure from my hand the best I could. But as I looked up and saw there was no easy way back up that cliff, I took it as a sign. It was then that I decided for good. There was no way I was going back. I threw away my distress flare then to ensure I didn't lose my nerve and send for help later.

I walked slowly in that early morning because it was dark and there were mine fields everywhere. I did what we called "night walk"—high, slow, deliberate steps designed not to hit a trip wire and set off a mine. At one point I saw a water-filled bomb crater topped over with ice. I chanced it that the ice was solid, but I was wrong and fell waist-deep into the muddy, cold water. I jumped to grab a root growing out of the side of the crater, pulled myself out, and kept going. Strangely, I didn't get much colder, because my pant legs froze almost instantly into hard cylinders that didn't touch my legs.

It was easy to get disoriented in the dark. At one point, as the sun came up, I looked at my compass again and realized I had been traveling almost an hour in the wrong direction and had to reverse course. I still had my M-14 rifle with me, but I had tied a white T-shirt I brought just for this purpose around the muzzle, to signal to anyone who saw me that I had no intention of shooting. (I found out later, however, that the North Koreans didn't even know what this signal meant.) I had also taken all the ammunition out of my rifle and put it in my ammo pouch, so that I could not be accused of crossing into North Korea with hostile intentions, thereby causing more trouble for the Americans I had left behind.

I have always felt bad, and continue to feel bad, about abandoning those men under my command. To abandon your troops is about the worst thing a military leader, which is what I was supposed to be, can do. Those soldiers, I knew, would stay on that hill, freezing, until dawn and after, waiting for me to return.

There is no doubt that January 5, 1965, was a time when I gave in to the very worst side of myself, when I attempted to run from all of my problems rather than confront them head-on like a man and a soldier. I let my men down, I let the U.S. Army down, I let the American people down, and I made it very difficult for my family in the United States to live a normal life, with the cloud of my actions hanging over them for so long. Over the next forty years, during the hell I often had to suffer in North Korea, I had a lot of time to think about my actions, and I apologized to those men, the American people, and my family a multitude of times in my thoughts. But now that I am able to do so in a way that maybe some of them can finally hear, I would like to say I am sorry to all of them again now. I don't know if any of them will accept my apology—I imagine some will and some won't—but I offer it anyway.

Not long after daylight, I saw a North Korean soldier behind a chest-high guard post on the other side of a ten-foot barbed and electrified wire fence. The winter wind was blowing so hard from the south that he had turned his back to the border and could not see me coming. I yelled out to him. When he turned, his eyes widened in that bug-eyed way you usually only see in cartoons. He must have pushed a silent alarm because although he did not say a word, eight or ten soldiers came running within seconds from a small house about fifty yards away over to a large gate that was just ten or so yards from the guard post. There was a brief moment of humor in even this, the most terrifying moment of my life, when the soldiers had to go running back to the house because they had forgotten the gate's key. Finally, they all came out and circled me with their rifles drawn. Though I was scared,

I knew in that moment that at least they weren't going to kill me. How did I know? Since they were in a circle, if one fired, the bullet would go through me and likely hit one of his comrades, too. In a matter of moments, they had grabbed me by the arms and took me into that small house. My life, as I had known it for twenty-four years, was over.

3 | Housemates

In the house on the border, they blindfolded me, searched me, and sat me down in a tiny room, more like an empty closet, really, about one yard by three yards, with a guard at the door. None of the eight or ten soldiers who would come in and out of the adjoining room spoke English, but I could catch the gist of some of the things they were saying just from their gestures. They were very curious about me. "Is he alone?" "Why did he come here?" And this was the biggest question as they inspected my M-14 and looked at the rounds in my ammo pouch: "Why is his weapon unloaded?" They just couldn't fathom it. There was a small fireplace, more like a covered brick stove, in the room, and they let me warm up by it. They brought me food, a simple rice stew, and told me, "Moga, moga." They gave me a drink that looked like rice paddy water, so I refused to drink it. I found out later that it was simply rice pot water—after cooking a pot of rice, you swish more hot water around the pot, scrape burned rice off the bottom, and pour it into a cup. This is a staple drink in North Korea. I would eventually become very familiar with it, even grow to like it, but at the time, I said, "Uh-uh. No way."

The man who was obviously the superior officer came into the room and looked me over. He could not speak English, either, but he wanted to know why my face was all bloody. He was clearly concerned that one of his men had laid an unauthorized beating on me, but I was able to make him understand that whatever had happened had happened before his men had gotten their hands on me. After that I sat there, saying nothing, no one saying anything to me, in that little room until afternoon.

As the afternoon wore on, some of the soldiers came in and put a blindfold on me, tied me up, and trundled me into a Russian jeep. A driver and a captain sat in the front, and two guards sat on either side of me in the back. We drove about an hour to a military base in Kaesong. Inside one of the buildings at the small base, they started interrogating me. It was just the basics: name, rank, serial number. The interpreter didn't know much English; he was reading out of a book. I got the feeling that they were just killing time, and I was right. Within an hour, we were back in the jeep and driving again.

After a five- or ten-minute drive, we pulled up at what looked like a private house. It was now about seven o'clock. There was a colonel there, along with seven or eight other uniformed North Koreans, and based on the way it was decorated, I guessed it was the colonel's private home or maybe a government guest house. They put me in a big room, about twelve tatami mats (so, about two hundred square feet total), with a big, long table and chairs. I was alone, and the room was cold. One of them brought me a dinner of rice soup and canned fish.

After dinner, they started in on what was more like a proper interrogation. They had finally found a translator who knew what
he was doing, for starters. The colonel was the main interrogator.
He would ask something in Korean, and the interpreter would ask
the same thing in English right after him: "Why did you come
here?" "Where is the rest of your unit?" "Who else is with you?"
"How did you make it across the DMZ?" Throughout the session,
he never raised his voice, and he never used a questioning tech-
nique even close to torture or coercion. As much as I hate to admit
it now, he was almost a gentleman. In my opinion, North Korea
was a lot stronger in a lot of ways then than it is today. Back in those
days, the military seemed like a real military, and they even seemed
to have a kind of dignity and pride in their professionalism. And
the whole economy wasn't that bad in those days. In those first few
years, it was obvious just from looking around that North Korea
was doing at least as well financially as South Korea. They were
our enemies, but they were enemies worthy of respect. Today, like
everything else in North Korea, the army has completely degener-
ated. The troops are starving along with the rest of the people. The
enlisted men are little more than kids in rags, and the officers are
totally corrupt. And no one knows the first thing about military
subjects anymore. The only thing about the North Korean Army
that we have to respect is the number of South Koreans and Americans they could kill if they ever decided they wanted to.

There was another officer in the room besides the colonel, the
translator, and a couple of guards. The other officer didn't say a
word, something I found unnerving, which was probably the
point. The colonel threw a number of maps at various levels of
magnification in front of me. "Where did you come from?"
"Where is your unit stationed?" "Where are there other units

stationed?" Here, I knew I was getting into territory that could put American lives at risk, but one of the best things I had going for me was that since I had only been in country for a few months, I honestly didn't know much.

I pointed to the mountain where my guard post, Guardpost Desart, was, but I didn't see any harm in that, since it was clearly visible by the North Koreans already. While on duty, I had often seen them through my binoculars looking at us through their binoculars. I even pointed out the locations of their loudspeakers on their side of the line that they used to blast propaganda and military music at us. That got them interested, when I pointed out Desart. "How tall is this mountain?" the colonel asked. I can't re-call the exact number now, but I replied whatever the real height was, so many thousand feet tall. The officer who hadn't spoken before jumped up and yelled what must have been "Liar!" in Korean, and he punched me square across the face. I started to gush blood again. "There is no mountain around here that tall," he continued through the interpreter. Obviously, he thought I gave him a height in meters, but I was not so handy with the met-ric system back then, so I couldn't covert it into a height he'd un-derstand. Finally, I got the interpreter to understand the problem enough to explain it. That interrogation lasted three or four hours. I thought I was there for the night, but at 11:30, they told me we were catching a train for Pyongyang.

The two guards, the captain who had been with me since the first jeep ride, and I boarded a regular train car. Five minutes after we sat down, the captain got up and made an announce-ment, and all of the civilians who had been sitting there got up and evacuated, so it was us four alone for the trip. At one point, I noticed that the guards, who were still carrying all of my weapons, were playing with the two grenades I had brought with me. I have never been so nervous in my life. They were a new style of grenade even for us, so I was certain the guards had never seen anything like them before, and I was worried that one of them would accidentally detonate one. So I tried to tell them, in super-slow English, about the pin, saying, "No touch that. Very dangerous." I don't know if they were offended, but this was not the way I planned on dying, so even though I was the prisoner, I didn't care. Eventually they stopped playing with the grenades, but it was probably as much because they got bored as it was because of my telling them not to. Relieved and finally able to relax, I fell asleep—the first sleep I had gotten in almost forty-eight hours. I didn't wake up until 5:30 A.M., when the train had already arrived in Pyongyang in an underground station.

After getting off the train, the captain, the two guards, and I waited about thirty minutes for a car to arrive. It was still dark outside, and there were no lights, so I couldn't see any of the city. We drove to a house about a third of a mile away from Kim Il-sung University, right in the center of the city. The house was small, only a few rooms, with heavy paper covering concrete floors and a fireplace outside that heated the house from underneath—a typical Korean heating system. The walls were whitewashed clay or cement. They put me in one of the rooms, and a woman brought me food—more simple rice stew. About thirty minutes later, a colonel came in and gave me trousers and a white shirt and took my uniform away.

I was in that house about ten or twelve days. I could not leave the room, except to use the toilet outside or the washbasin in an adjoining room. The lighting was naked overhead bulbs that I was not allowed to turn off, even when I was sleeping. Late that first week, however, they took me into town to get a haircut and a bath. During my time in that first house, two people in civilian clothes came and interrogated me every day from eight or nine in the morning until four or five in the afternoon. I don't think they were all that qualified to do interrogations, and I again got the feeling that they were killing time until they figured out where they really wanted to put me. Maybe they knew already from the guys who questioned me earlier that I didn't know anything useful about positions and placements of American forces. I hadn't been on any field problems, for example, and I told them so. They did, however, want to know a lot about inspections. How often did we have them? How long did we prepare for them? How long did they take? What were officers looking for, and what got you penalized? I didn't know if they were just looking for ways to improve their own drills or if they were planning on infiltrating one of our units by having a North Korean pose as one of the Republic of Korea Army troops who sometimes used to train with us. The interrogators then wanted to know a lot about my weapons, which was more understandable. How does the M-14's automatic selector switch work? What is the blast radius of the hand grenades? Realizing that the answers to all of these questions had the potential to put American lives at risk, I did my best to answer them as incompetently as I could without arousing their suspicion.

At the end of those ten or twelve days, the colonel reappeared and told me to get my things together quickly: I was moving in with three other U.S. servicemen who had walked across the DMZ. I knew who they were already. All along the South Korean side of the DMZ, these guys—Private First Class Larry Allen Abshier, Private James Joseph Dresnok, and Specialist

Jerry Wayne Parrish—were notorious the way I assumed I now was. The colonel and I got into another jeep—I noticed that I was no longer being very heavily guarded, if at all (I guess they figured, "Where is he going to go?")—and drove about ten minutes to a neighborhood called Saedong.

We pulled up to a little brick house, and Dresnok and Parrish were waiting for me. Abshier wasn't there. He was in the hospital for colitis and wouldn't rejoin the house until the late summer. We all introduced ourselves and started talking. I was starved for anyone who could speak English, and they were also happy to have another person to break up the boredom. Just like the North Korean interrogators, they, too, were full of questions. The first thing they wanted to know was why I came over. They were all enlisted men who were in trouble with the army, and they couldn't imagine why a sergeant who wasn't already up for some sort of court-martial would cross the DMZ. I told them I didn't want to go to Vietnam. Dresnok shook his head at that one and just said, "Well, you may have had one foot in the pot, but you just jumped in the fire." We all got along okay that first night. We assumed (as we almost always did) that everything we said was being recorded, but they were so hungry for anything new in their lives that after I ran out of world events to tell them about and after trying to figure out how many people we knew in common, I stayed up all night telling them every single joke I could remember.

The next Saturday, one of the North Koreans in charge walked me to the hospital to meet Abshier. We talked for about thirty minutes, and I'll never forget that one of the first things Abshier asked me was if I had any money, because they had a little shop in the hospital where he wanted to buy some things. I told him I didn't have any money, which was the truth. Abshier would wind up becoming my closest friend of the three, but I came away from that first meeting shaking my head at what a strange, simple, and disconnected man he was.

I didn't know it at the time, but those three men would, for better and worse, be permanent fixtures of my entire time in North Korea. I got to know them all better than I have known just about anybody else in my life. All four of us were similar in a lot of ways. We were all young, dumb soldiers from poor backgrounds who wouldn't have had anything if it weren't for the army, but then we threw that away too by running away from varying degrees of real or imagined trouble rather than confronting our problems head-on. If there was an odd man out, though, it was me. I was slightly older; I was a noncommissioned officer while they were enlisted men; and I had a pretty good military record while the other three were pretty much total fuck-ups as soldiers. The way they described it, Abshier and Dresnok were running from the law. They were each up for a serious court-martial before they crossed. Parrish's reasons were more personal, and he didn't elaborate about them much except to say that if he ever went home, his father-in-law would kill him. The three of them, also like me, walked across the DMZ without really thinking about the huge consequences of what they were doing and without understanding what North Korea was really like. None of them intended to stay in North Korea, and none of them were communist sympathizers. All of them assumed that they would be able to get out one way or another, and they experienced a rude shock when it dawned on them that they were trapped, forever, in North Korea. All of them quickly grew to hate the country and would have left in a second if they could have.

Over the ensuing decades, sometimes we were the closest of friends, and sometimes we were the bitterest of enemies. Sometimes we could count on each other for support against the insanity of North Korea, while at other times the insanity itself would encourage us to turn against each other. At first we were housemates, struggling just to stay alive and sane during frequent periods of cold, hunger, and despair. And decades later, when we all had started families of our own, we formed a strange, insular little community of foreigners in the world's most strange, insular, and foreign society. What a sorry-ass little foursome we were when I stop to think about it.

That Saedong house was the first of many places I lived in North Korea over the next forty years. We only stayed there for about six months. It was a simple brick house with two bedrooms. Whichever government official was watching us took one bedroom. We Americans shared the other bedroom, which was only about six mats big (or about one hundred square feet) and had three desks crammed into it. We slept on the floor any way we could manage, and it was a tight fit. Other than that, there was a room for the cook, a kitchen, and a dining room with a table and chairs that we were not allowed to use. (We ate our meals in our bedroom or outside if the weather was nice.) The dining room sometimes housed extra military officers whenever they showed up. The toilet was outside, and there was only cold running water in the house, but the running water rarely worked, so usually we had to fetch water from the well, too. The whole house was surrounded by a six-and-a-half-foot-high wood fence, and there was a guard stationed in a crow's nest atop a telephone pole outside.

Like every other North Korean household, we were assigned a leader. I had too many leaders to count over forty years. As members of the North Korean Workers' Party (which we usually just called "the Organization"), leaders were responsible for keeping an eye on our every move, making sure we behaved and that we lived according to "correct ideology." Depending on where I was living and with whom, the leader (or leaders) would sometimes live in the same house as I, while at other times he would live in a house nearby. A leader's contact with me was nearly constant, especially at the beginning, and even in later years, rarely a day went by that I didn't see, talk to, get criticized by, or get into a fight with my leader. Leaders oversaw our propaganda indoctrination—the hours of forced study and memorization of Kim Il-sung's teaching that we endured—and they administered the special self-criticism sessions we underwent whenever they believed that we had committed some sort of infraction, as well as the regularly scheduled self-criticism sessions held once a week.

Self-criticism is a way of life in North Korea. Everybody has to do it, even the highest party members. Our sessions were once a week on Monday mornings. All through the week, we were supposed to keep a diary, where we wrote about the times we failed to live up to Kim Il-sung's teachings. Perhaps we left the house one day without permission, or perhaps the front door broke because we had not tended to its upkeep well enough—both of those would be good entries for the diary. Then we used those diary entries for our criticism. There are variations to the self-criticism session, but basically you stand at attention and confess all your failings to those superiors present. The weekly sessions, which we called "sum up," were pretty formulaic, and once we got the hang of it, they were not that difficult, though they could get extremely stressful when a leader decided to prove a point and got in your face and yelled at you for hours on end. Even so, the key is to detach your mind from the experience as much as possible, to treat it as if none of the words that you are saying and none of the proceedings you are participating in have any meaning at all—which happens to be the truth.

Usually, you started by citing a teaching of Kim Il-sung's, something like: "Our Great Leader Kim Il-sung taught as follows. The first and foremost task of a revolutionary is to study. If the revolutionary fails to study properly, he will fail to successfully create the revolution." Some of these teaching-recitations could go on for a few minutes, and you better not screw up even a single word or you'd have to start over or get in more trouble. After that, you would read your failings from your sum-up book. My self-criticism formula was almost always to admit to not being as diligent about studying as I should have been. There were a lot of Monday mornings when we realized we hadn't kept our diaries, so we would scramble to remember things we had done wrong. Often we'd just invent them or copy them from previous weeks. Other times, we would do something we knew we weren't supposed to, like steal some peaches, and we'd say, "That's one for the sum-up book." After reading all the things you did wrong, you'd express regret that your revolutionary ideology was not sufficiently honed or whatever to uphold Kim Il-sung's teachings, and then you'd say you were sorry you let the party and Kim Il-sung down. And finally, you'd finish by listing all the ways through more committed thinking and conduct you were going to do better next time. Once a month, we had to submit a written confession, at least four pages long. And any time we did something the cadres considered serious, we could be called in for a special session.

Leaders never operated independently, though. In North Korea, even the watchers were being watched. A chief of staff was the leader in charge of the leaders of a small group of families or homes. He was the boss of the leaders and drivers. (Leaders usually had cars.) And the chiefs of staff always had at least a superior or two above them, simply called "cadres," who would come around intermittently to check up both on us and on the leader.

Some leaders would be major recurring presences in my life over many decades. Other leaders would last for only a few weeks and I would never see them again. Sometimes we would call a leader by name, although this was rare, since we soon came to assume that the names they gave us were fakes. Sometimes you would meet Comrade Pak, and the very next week the exact same man would introduce himself as Comrade Lee, as if you were some sort of moron and wouldn't notice. Even if they were telling the truth, however, since this was Korea, almost everybody you met had the same four or five names anyway—Lee, Kim, Pak, Moon, and so forth. So for most of those who stuck around longer than a few weeks, we developed nicknames: the Tall Cadre, Whitey, the Fat Cadre, the Colonel in Glasses, and so on.

Two or three of these leaders became the closest thing I would ever have to a North Korean friend, and they would take great risks to help me out when I was in trouble. But they were the exceptions. Many leaders were just cowards pretending to be thugs—they could be easily manipulated or bought off. Others were cruel bastards who hated me and the other Americans so deeply that they refused to see us as human and enjoyed making our lives hell. I, in turn, learned to hate these bastards right back.

Most were just pathetic—a combination of small-time power and big-time fear. One of these idiots was the officer who was my escort from the border to Pyongyang the day I crossed over. We ultimately nicknamed him Captain Major. Why Captain Major? Because sometimes he would show up wearing a captain's uniform, and sometimes he would be wearing a major's. One time I asked him about his uniforms and told him how confusing it was that he seemed to hold two ranks at the same time. He responded, "That's right, and someday I'll make colonel!" Later, I would think about him, hoping that he did "make colonel" and that someone, somewhere is now referring to him as Captain Major Colonel.

Starting here in this little house and throughout the rest of the next forty years, I had to adapt to live in a place that I came to think of as another planet. Years later, in fact, I would often tell my daughters, "We are not in the world. This is not the real world." They had no idea what I was talking about until we ultimately got out. The rules of logic, order, and cause-and-effect ceased to apply. Things happened all the time that made no sense and for which we were given no explanation. Why did a squad of ten soldiers just drive up in a truck and set up camp in our backyard? We didn't know, and they wouldn't say. Who are they, where did they come from, and what are they doing here? Again, no answers, either from them or our leader. They would then stay for a few days or a few weeks, you never knew how long, and then, one day, with no reason offered, they would just pack up and leave. Or we would be told to do something, to weave some fishing nets, say, "for the good of the party and the people." Just a few days later, we would be told to drop that, since we were being moved because the Organization needed our house more, apparently, than the fishing nets. Sometimes the person telling us what to do would be our leader, and sometimes he would be a cadre we had never seen before and would never see again. You just never knew.

For much of my forty years, it is true that I enjoyed a high amount of freedom and material comfort considering that starvation, malnutrition, slave labor, and execution or imprisonment without trial are standard risks for huge parts of the population in North Korea. It was never easy for me there, and in most other countries, my existence would have qualified as the lowest of the low. But in North Korea, I and those I was with usually had enough food to eat and a roof over our heads, which in that twisted realm made me one of the fortunate few. We four who willingly walked across the DMZ were cold war trophies, which is why I think we were never held like POWs and why, I believe, we were kept mostly healthy. As the stars of several propaganda pamphlets—and later movies—we had to look like we were happy, or at least healthy. With permission and supervision, we were allowed to leave the house fairly regularly and shop in the Pyongyang Shop, a store that was reserved only for foreigners, or go fishing if we had passed our studies and finished whatever work detail was laid out for us.

But still, I suffered from enough cold, hunger, beatings, and mental torture to frequently make me wish I was dead. To this day, I suffer from panic attacks, high blood pressure, and insomnia. It is hard to convey how hopeless we were during much of that time. Sometimes we took chances that seem unbelievable to me now—whether stealing government property, mouthing off to the cadres, or going on daredevil hikes, clinging to tiny ledges on the sides of canyons, "just for fun"—because in many ways we felt like we were already dead. Other times, when we participated in what seems like the worst forms of betrayal to the United States—whether acting in propaganda movies or teaching military cadets English—it is similarly difficult to express how futile we had come to believe resistance was, how impossible escape.

Rationing is one of the primary ways of distributing goods in North Korea, and during our early years, our rations went something like this: Every month we got a tube of toothpaste, a bar of body soap, a bar of clothing soap, a pair of socks, two bottles of beer, and forty packs of cigarettes. That may sound like a lot of smokes, but these cigarettes were the worst quality I have ever seen. They must have been stuffed with corn husks rather than tobacco. You had to wet them, like they were roll-your-owns, because if you didn't, when you lit one, it would burn up toward your fingers before your very eyes before you even took a puff. You were lucky if you got more than three drags off a single cigarette. Every Sunday we were taken into town for a bath and a haircut. At first we were also issued a straight razor once a month, until I told a leader I particularly disliked that a straight razor would come in handy during a fight. After that, we were issued safety razors. Starting out, we each got paid five won per month. A won at that time was worth about fifty U.S. cents. A pack of 555 brand Western cigarettes was about two won at the Pyongyang Shop, so I would usually buy two packs of those and try to make them last all month.

Our primary "job" at first was to study. They had lots of propaganda books in English. We were ordered to read all day about North Korean history, famous tales of the guerillas who battled the Japanese during World War II, and the teachings of Kim Il-sung. The books had names like *The People's Leader* and *Among the People*. We were supposed to read them and then tell our leader what we had learned. It was like an oral book report from school. If you passed, you got to move on to another book. If you didn't pass, you had to read the book again. Our other task was to teach English to the military officers who would come in and out of the house in packs of four or five for anywhere from a few days to a few weeks at a time. They weren't really English lessons. They were more like conversation classes. We never really knew who they were, and we were never able to determine any pattern to their schedules.

Until we all got married, we usually had a cook to make our meals. This sounds like we were living the high life, but having a cook was no luxury, I assure you. The cook was more often than not just another set of Organization eyes or another person you had to worry about stealing from you. The food she made was an afterthought: It was almost always too little and barely edible. The rice was filled with bugs, the vegetables were wormy, and the meat, if there was any meat at all, was often spoiled.

In June of 1965, a cadre arrived to tell us that the Organization needed our house—which was in a prime location in east Pyongyang—for some other purpose, so we were being moved to a bigger and better house in Mangyongdae, about thirty minutes away. Mangyongdae is still very close to central Pyongyang and is famous throughout North Korea as the ancestral homeland of Kim Il-sung's family. The house we were moved into was high on a hilltop and definitely bigger, big enough that Parrish and I were able to have our own room while Dresnok and Abshier shared a room. We also got beds. The leaders' area, which was two large rooms, had its own entrance. Off to one side of the house was the Ping-Pong room, so dubbed because it had an old Ping-Pong table in the middle of it. We used the room as our study and the table as a desk. (It was a pretty uncomfortable one, too. Sitting on a regular chair, the table came up to my armpits.) One time, some officers came back with some paddles and built a "net" by laying a stick across two bricks set on either side of the center of the table, but that was the only time I ever saw anybody play Ping-Pong there.

This house was bigger, but it was by no means better. It had no heat and no running water. We had to go one hundred fifty yards down the hill with two buckets on a yoke to fetch the drinking water. Even though the Taedong and Potong Rivers ran nearby, we couldn't do anything with that water, since they dumped sewage in the river just a few miles upstream. At first, we didn't have any buckets, so we borrowed buckets from an army unit nearby that was growing corn. That lasted a few weeks until we noticed that the army was using those same buckets to fertilize their corn with shit from their own latrine. "But we wash out the buckets!" they claimed, when we told them how disgusting that was. We weren't having any of that. We made the leader get us some of our own buckets. During the winter, however, the well would dry up or freeze up completely. When that happened, we would try to cut ice or melt snow if there was any. A couple of times, when there was no snow and dying of thirst became a real possibility, they had to bring Russian-made water tanker trucks with emergency drinking water.

At this house, they moved us on to more advanced studies. We graduated from simple tales of history and freedom fighters to more complicated passages on the Juche Idea, or Kimilsungism, which was Kim Il-sung's homegrown theory of communism. Juche's biggest message was absolute self-reliance. North Koreans doing everything themselves was better, according to Kim Il-sung's theory, than relying even on other communist countries like China and the Soviet Union for trade. I'm no economist, but it is a crazy theory. And the more you study it, the less sense it makes. Sometimes, I would look around, and I couldn't believe that a whole nation seemed to believe this gibberish. And of course it was all horseshit anyway, because any fool could see that not only would North Korea collapse without trade with other countries, but that it also relied on a steady stream of handouts and gifts just to feed itself.

People always ask me if I think I was brainwashed, or they ask how long it took me to undo all the propaganda I absorbed. I can honestly say that I was never brainwashed, and all four of us Americans never bought into any of the phony history, economics, social theory, and Kim Il-sung worship that they shoved down our throats. I can't tell you why, except to say that it all looked as heavy-handed and ridiculous to us from the inside as it does from the outside. They didn't use any of the sophisticated brainwashing and mind control tricks you see in the movies, though I am not sure those work in real life anyway. All they did to us four was make us study and memorize and conduct self-criticism endlessly. In the end, the never-ending drudgery made us less receptive to what they were trying to convince us of rather than more. Perhaps if you are Korean, and especially if you had been brought up this way, it might be possible to believe all, or at least most, of what they tell you, but since we were brought up knowing the outside world, we knew it was all lies, and we didn't start thinking it was the truth simply because they insisted it was.

We studied about ten or eleven hours a day. If we didn't memorize enough or were not able to recite portions of our studies on demand, we were forced to study sixteen hours a day on Sunday, which was usually our only day of rest. And if one of us failed, we all were punished. Early on, the passages we were supposed to memorize were in English. But then they moved us toward memorizing the passages in Korean, even though most of us didn't know Korean. (At first, the Organization didn't want us to learn Korean, thinking that it was better for us not to know what was going on, and before I arrived, they even went so far as to teach the others a bogus Korean alphabet. After a while, however, they realized we were going to wind up learning Korean, or at least how to speak Korean, no matter what they did, so they relented and decided to teach us regular grammar and reading.) Until I really learned the language, however, I would have to memorize passages phonetically, writing out every syllable in English letters, memorizing everything by sound rather than meaning. To this day, I can recite more Korean propaganda than you could ever hope to hear, in both English and Korean. Sometimes, I think, I recite it in my sleep.

It was during this time that I also really began to understand how important the personality cult of Kim Il-sung was. One time I asked some cadres, "What happens when Kim Il-sung dies?" This was long before Kim Jong-il was the appointed successor, but that is beside the point. I thought it was an innocent and reasonable question. But at that time, to even suggest that Kim Il-sung was going to die like a mere mortal was unthinkable. I caught all kinds of hell for that one. Parrish and Dresnok told me that they thought I got off easy since I had only been in the country for less than a year. If they had asked the same thing, they said, they would have been severely beaten or even sent to prison.

While we were at Mangyongdae, sometimes the leaders would disappear for days or weeks at a time. We were always left in the care of army officers, who still came by in groups of four or five for English lessons, but the officers were more lenient than the leaders. They didn't care what we did as long as they were learning English, so we had more time for "freedalisms," which was our word for doing things without permission. There was an old Columbia hi-fi in the Ping-Pong room, and the reception dial actually worked. On it, we could pick up Voice of America and Armed Forces Network, Japan. When no one was around, we would sneak into the Ping-Pong room and listen to the news or a Western radio drama. It took them about a year before they caught on, came in, and modified the radio so that it only picked up Pyongyang Radio Broadcasting Channel 1 and Channel 2.

Soon after we moved into this house, Abshier finally came back from the hospital. Almost as soon as he did, Dresnok started in on him, preying on Abshier's weakness. Dresnok would throw his clothes around and tell Abshier to pick them up or to wash them. And Abshier would. That was just the way their two personalities were. Dresnok, who was nearly six and a half feet tall and more than two hundred fifty pounds, was a natural-born bully accustomed to getting his way. Abshier, on the other hand, was a simple, sweet, good-hearted soul who was also more than a little dumb and easy to take advantage of. One time on that old Columbia hi-fi, we heard a radio drama of the John Steinbeck book *Of Mice and Men,* which was about a simpleton named

Lennie. After that, Parrish and Dresnok would often call Abshier "Lennie." They would laugh themselves silly over that.
"Hey, Lennie!" they would yell.

I didn't like any of this. I told Abshier that he had to stand up
for himself and quit being pushed around by Dresnok. So one
day, Dresnok was giving him his same old shit, and Abshier refused to wash Dresnok's clothes. Dresnok made a move on Abshier, but I stepped in and beat Dresnok down. I threw the first
punch, I admit it, but I whooped his ass. That was the last time
Dresnok bothered Abshier in that way, but it was the beginning
of a long and turbulent relationship between me and Dresnok,
one that often involved spilled blood, usually mine.

One time, we traded dozens of rationed socks we had saved
with someone in town for a little boat we hoped to use for fishing. It had so many holes in it that it was almost worthless, but
across the river, the North Korean government was building an
electrical plant. In the middle of the night, the four of us took the
boat across the river, snuck into the power plant past several
armed guards, and stole a bag of coal tar to repair our boat. We
crawled past the guards with the bag of coal tar on our backs,
passing the bag from man to man when one of us became too
tired. We used the coal tar to repair the boat, which we then used
for fishing in the middle of the night. That was a risky one, since
to steal something from the North Korean government is pun-
ishable by death, but we were so bored and crazy that we honestly didn't care.

Another time when the leaders were gone, we snuck up into
the attic to see if we could scrounge some old electrical insulators
to weight down a fishing net we were making. When we were up
in the attic, we found microphones everywhere, pointing into

every room. We found the recording deck under the leader's bed later that day. Parrish collected all the microphones and buried them in our backyard. When our leader at that time, Major Kim, got back, Parrish told the leader that he could have the microphones back if he took him into Pyongyang to buy some wine. Major Kim could have had us all shot for this, of course, but the blackmail worked because he was more worried about his own neck and all the trouble he would be in for allowing such a violation to happen.

Around the spring of 1966, we started having trouble with our rations. We stopped getting as many razors and as much soap. And then the food supplies started to dwindle. We suspected that our leader at the time, Leader Kim (a different guy than Major Kim), was in cahoots with the ration supply guys to skim off of the top of our stuff, figuring there was nothing we could do about it. In the spring, the supply guy came up and said, "Due to shortages, there are no more canned meat rations." But he had a hog with him that he said that we could have. If we fattened it up for winter, he said, we could butcher it and keep the meat for ourselves. So all that summer and fall, we worked like hell to fatten that hog up. We fed it fish and fish heads, tons of grass, anything we could find. By late fall, that hog was up to about two hundred pounds, and we were just waiting for it to get cold so that the meat we butchered didn't spoil too quickly. Before that could happen, however, a bunch of cadres came and butchered that hog in our own yard, right in front of our eyes, and carted it off, saying the Organization needed it.

Abshier was so mad he called the Organization a *ga-sicki*. The word means "dog," but it is about the worst Korean insult imaginable. Everything screeched to a halt. The cadres went to a guesthouse about three hundred yards away where a bunch of soldiers were staying and brought three of them back with their rifles. They pinned Abshier against a wall and lined up fifty yards away from him. They said they were going to execute him right there if he didn't apologize. Abshier was shaking and his voice was trembling, but he managed to squeak out that he was sorry for calling the Organization a dog. Through it all, I wasn't all that worried that they were actually going to kill him. At one point a leader had told me that Kim Il-sung himself had declared us valuable, saying that one American was worth one hundred Koreans. After I heard that, I no longer thought that they would kill us without a good reason. But I know it was easier for me to keep that attitude than Abshier on that day since I wasn't staring down the barrels of three AK-47s. I think it really shook up Abshier.

Still, for us, the episode was enough to make us try to do something. Our rations were so low that we were going days without food, and our own attempts at farming and raising animals weren't enough to make up the difference. One afternoon, when we weren't being watched, we went into Pyongyang and went straight to the Workers' Party Headquarters. They found an English speaker to talk to us, and we told them that our rations were being stolen by Leader Kim. Of course, they had already called Leader Kim the second we arrived, so he showed up in no time, carted us back home, and gave us round-the-clock studies and extra self-criticism sessions.

A few months later, we went to Pyongyang a second time with the intention of complaining to the Workers' Party. The second we sat down and started explaining ourselves, the guy listening to us excused himself. We smelled a rat. We knew he was calling Leader Kim, so we said, "Let's get out of here." We hustled outside, and there, down the road, we saw the Russian embassy. All this time, I should explain, I had never given up my original plan of trying to get a diplomatic transfer through the Soviet Union back to the United States. By now I had figured out that North Korea was going to do everything it could to prevent that from happening, but I was still holding out for my chance to explain my plight to the Russians. And here it was.

We hightailed it over to the embassy, where we walked right in, no doubt because the Korean and Russian guards assumed we were Russians. Once there, we asked for political asylum. Taken aback, the front desk employee found a translator for us, and he and a diplomat took us into a private room where they listened to our story for more than two hours. He gave us Russian cigarettes and cups of some of the best coffee we had had in ages. Since there were no ashtrays, he told us to stab out the butts in the fine china coffee saucers. I don't know if he was pretending, but he seemed sympathetic and serious. We felt good about what was taking place. He told us that he needed to talk to Moscow and that he would be right back. He was gone over an hour. When he returned, he said, "I am sorry, but there is nothing we can do for you, and you are going to have to leave and never come back." We filed out quietly and returned home, not saying a word.

After the Russian embassy incident, three of us concluded, finally, that there was no way out of North Korea and we were going to die there. Parrish, however, held out hope longer than the rest of us and was always trying to concoct schemes for getting out. Once, he tried a solo bid for asylum at the Chinese embassy, but he got turned down there, too. He had ideas about trekking north through the mountains to China or building a raft to float down a river and out to sea. None would have worked, and they never got past the talking stage. For North Korean refugees, it is nearly impossible to escape. And for Westerners as conspicuous as us, we concluded that it was doubly so.

In the fall of 1967, Pyongyang flooded, so officials from the Organization came and said they needed our house. We moved to a new house in Daeyang-ri. It was more remote than the last house, more than an hour drive down a dirt road from the nearest turnoff. It was a nice house, with many small rooms. Again, the leaders were gone for days and weeks at a time, but now we didn't even have officers coming by for English lessons, so we were mostly just left by ourselves for a few months until a colonel who stopped by learned by chance from one of us that we knew how to make fishing nets.

A few days later, he showed up with forty-four pounds of nylon string and said the Organization needed our nets. That was a bit of a benefit, I suppose, being given so much nylon, considering that usually we scavenged our nylon from the linings of old automobile tires. But we quickly came to hate being given so much nylon, since it seemed like the whole time we were there that all we did was make fishing nets. Once you get good at it, it is not difficult to weave the one-inch holes with your little bamboo needle, but it is hard on your eyes and hard on your back. They told us that we had to make five hundred meters (about 550 yards) of net. And we had to do it in about a year's time. That was almost impossible, but we did it.

We had learned to improvise some of the materials we didn't have. Back in the previous house, we would scavenge lead from old car batteries, melting and shaping the sinkers ourselves to weigh down the bottom of the nets. But here, we didn't have a junkyard nearby, so we made the sinkers out of clay that we would harden in a fire. Likewise, back at the old house, we actually had enough access to wine bottles to make the floats for the top of the net out of real corks. Here, we had to cut the floats from pine bark instead. We had become experts in backwoods fishing wisdom, such as this: What is the secret ingredient to toughen up your nylon net, transforming it from something that will last for a few seasons into something that will last for a few decades? Pig's blood. After you have finished weaving your net, take the whole thing and soak it in a vat of fresh pig's blood. (Yes, a few gallons of pig's blood can be hard to find, but the benefits are great enough that it is worth befriending a butcher, or buying and killing your own pig, or doing whatever it takes.) Once the nylon fibers are thoroughly soaked, let the net dry in the sun. After it is dry, steam the whole net on a stove in a large pot partially filled with water. (Keep the net out of the water by placing it on a few pieces of wood inside the pot itself.) Once the blood has fully cooked into the nylon, take the net out and let it dry again. When you are done, the net will be shiny, black, slick, resistant to snags, and very strong.

Near our house, there were a bunch of other houses. They were all off-limits. A leader told us, "See that road? Don't go down it. See that house? Don't go near it." We didn't know who lived there, but we guessed they were filled with Republic of Korea Army prisoners. One day, Abshier and I were at our house. Dresnok and Parrish were at the lake, which was about three hundred yards away over a hill. About a week or two before, we had seen the army digging a hole on the side of the mountain. Dresnok and Parrish came back and said, "Hey, the hole is now a bald spot of dirt. Let's go check it out." We walked over there, and a dog was digging up the fresh dirt. That's when we saw them: two dead human feet sticking right up out of the ground. We didn't believe what we were seeing, but we took a closer look, and sure enough, there was no mistaking it. From the size of the grave, about two by five yards, it could have held five to ten people, depending on how deep it was. We decided to get the hell out of there and leave it alone. We swore we would never tell what we saw. A few days later, however, we saw a woman running down the hill from where the grave was. She was screaming her head off, and we knew exactly what it was all about. A little while later, people from the army came around and killed every dog in the neighborhood.

In January of 1968, we heard on the news that North Korea had captured an American surveillance ship called the U.S.S. *Pueblo.* A group of cadres came by a few days later just to brief us about it. They were boasting. They gave us a pamphlet in English they had already printed up, titled, "Aggressive American Spy Ship Captured by the Heroic North Korean People's Navy," or something like that. In the text of the pamphlet, it said that the ship had been "captured on the high seas." We knew when we read it that they probably didn't want to be saying that since they would have had no right to board another country's ship in international waters. And sure enough, they came back a few days later with a new pamphlet exactly the same as the old one, except with that phrase taken out.

Contrary to some rumors and accusations that have been aimed at me, I had nothing to do with the *Pueblo* incident. None of us four Americans had anything to do with the *Pueblo* whatsoever. Not only did we not participate in any interrogation of the *Pueblo*'s crew, we never met any of them or even laid eyes on any of them. There is no way the North Koreans would have trusted us enough to go anywhere near that boat, let alone speak to the sailors. All we knew about the fate of the *Pueblo* was the boastful propaganda that the Korean news would run throughout the year until the crew was released in December. And since then, of course, a one-sided presentation of the *Pueblo* incident has become a favorite part of anti-American North Korean history and lore. (When the North Koreans made a movie about the incident in 1992, I played the captain of the aircraft carrier U.S.S. *Enterprise,* which was dispatched to the region at the height of the crisis.)

While the *Pueblo* was dominating the news in 1968, a leader named Major Han showed up, and we resumed our studies. In March of 1969, we moved again, to a house in Hwachon, which was about twenty miles outside of Pyongyang. This house was a dump. It was only two big rooms, and the walls and floors were pounded mud. There was barely enough room for four beds, so we got rid of the beds and slept on the floor. One night when we were sleeping, it was raining hard, and one of the walls of the house simply collapsed—it just fell away. Rain was blowing in all night, so all four of us crept to the other side of the room, trying to keep dry. The next day, as we were repairing the wall, some farmers offered to help. They started building the wall by stacking cinder blocks one on top of another and then pushing the towers of blocks as close to each other as possible. When we showed them that the wall would stand a lot better if they interlocked the bricks in rows rather than stacking them in columns, they acted like that was the most brilliant thing they had ever seen in their lives.

After moving to Hwachon, a cadre came by to tell us that the five won we were getting every month was being suspended indefinitely. Around this time as well, Major Han and others started dropping hints about us becoming citizens and entering society. They said that if we continued to study well (which was hilarious, since we were the worst students of all time), we could someday be more free. As part of this process, they had us write our autobiographies. My life story came out to one hundred forty-three handwritten pages. Dresnok's and Parrish's were about the same. Abshier, in typical fashion, topped five hundred pages and would have kept going if we hadn't told him that the North Koreans really don't care what types of artwork adorn the walls of Chicago's Union Station or whatever the hell he was going on and on about.

Our house was exactly ninety yards from the river. We had to carry so much water back to the house that we measured it. Another fifty yards downstream was a worksite for a nearby prison. Just about every day guards would bring work details of ten or twelve people at a time to dig sand for cement. The prisoners dressed in rags, got almost no food, and received brutal physical abuse from the guards. Guards would make the prisoners line up on their knees and kowtow to them to receive a single cigarette. Then the guards would hand them a cigarette and a single match. If they could not light the cigarette off of one match strike (and North Korean matches are horrible), then they just blew their chance for the day. But this passed for easy time in North Korea. This prison was not for the worst offenders. It was for people who had, say, fought with a work team leader or expressed doubt about the government (as opposed to criticizing it). The people there could reasonably expect to be released someday after their ideological reeducation was deemed a success.

Often we would head down to the work site to see if the guards had any kerosene, gasoline, or cigarettes they were willing to barter. On New Year's Day of 1971, we headed down there to see if they had anything new. Since it was a holiday, the medium-sentence prisoners were given a rare day off, so the guards filled the work detail with harder-luck, long-term inmates who were in for serious crimes against the government, like trying to escape North Korea or criticizing the government. Crimes like that were usually given a fifteen-year sentence, but the work was so brutal, it was as good as a death sentence, and everybody knew it. All four of us were heading up the riverbank when one of the guards we knew started blowing a whistle while he turned to us and waved us away. At the same time, we saw one of the prisoners running the other direction. We headed back toward home double time, but not before we heard a rifle shot ring out and saw two more guards head slowly in the direction the inmate had headed. The next day, with the regular prisoners digging as usual, we came back to the guard and asked him what happened. "He was making a run for it," said the guard, "so we stopped him." "Did you take him to the hospital?" we asked. "The hospital?" he laughed. "Hell, no." "What did you do to him?" we asked. "We took him back to the prison and made him dig his own grave," he said. "Then we shot him."

In 1971, some cadres showed up unexpectedly at our house with two Japanese men. I think the first one's name was Osada. He was stocky like a welder and had gold teeth. The second one's name I do not know. The cadres told us that these Japanese were going to live there from now on. None of us were too excited about that, not because we didn't like them—we didn't know them—but because of the crowding. That night, the Japanese told us they were on a merchant ship bound for South Korea when they encountered engine trouble. So they got into a smaller boat to go for help while the rest of the crew radioed in. But, they told us, their smaller boat's engine went out, so they drifted for a few days, and when they hit land, they were in North Korea, not South, and the Organization, believing them to be spies, wouldn't let them out.

The next day, however, there had been some change of plans. Maybe the Organization decided us mixing together wasn't such a good idea after all, since leaders showed up and carted the two Japanese men away. We never saw them again. Their story sounded pretty suspicious to us, too, and we Americans concluded they were probably spies of one sort or another, but on whose side, we had no idea.

Toward the end of 1971 and beginning of 1972, the cadres really stepped up our studies. They told us if we studied hard, they would give us our own houses, real jobs, an opportunity to fraternize with women, all of these things. We couldn't care less about the citizenship—in fact, none of us wanted it—but women, houses, and a "normal" life (which itself is something of a joke in North.Korea), those seemed like things worth working for. The Fifth Workers' Party Congress had happened in the fall of 1970, and we had to memorize all of the goals and achievements that came out of that meeting. They were planning on putting electricity and running water in all houses nationwide, for example. They gave us a booklet of about one hundred pages, and we had to memorize everything in it, word for word. It was in question-and-answer format, and we had to be ready for any question. Some of the answers went on for a paragraph or two. Some went on for pages and pages. What is the main task for agriculture? What is the main task for industry? How will the people accomplish party goals for electricity? coal? hydroelectric power? How will the party improve women's rights? Every day, I would go outside in the cold and read the answers out loud to myself. It was the only way I could learn. Finally, a cadre came to the house around March of 1972 and laid about fifty questions facedown on the table. Each of us had to pick three and give our answers.

I guess we all passed, because on June 30, a guy we called the Tall Cadre showed up and said that thanks to the benevolence of Kim Il-sung, we had been granted North Korean citizenship. "What if we don't take it?" I asked. He lowered his head, looked over at me from under his eyebrows, and said, "Then you won't be here tomorrow." I took that as a threat that I would be banished to Kumok-ri, a remote area that was legendary as one giant prison, rather than executed, but I did not know what would happen, and I did not take the risk of finding out either way. I accepted the citizenship without another word. Citizenship papers in North Korea at the time were booklets, like passports, but smaller. The pages had your photo, date of birth, registration number, occupation, and affiliation. My booklet said I was an office worker with the Peaceful Unification Committee. That was news to me.

4 | Cooks, Cadets, and Wives

Although none of us really wanted citizenship, our lives did get a bit better after we had it. We were never actually put into regular society, though (not that we realistically thought we would be). But, for starters, not only was our pay reinstated, but we also got a raise from five to ten won per month. Additionally, we each received our own homes, as had been promised. They were still modest places. They each had two four-mat rooms and a kitchen. Like almost all of the houses I have ever lived in, they had unreliable electricity, no hot running water, a coal-burning floor heating system, and no indoor bathroom.

But before we moved, they gave us one final surprise: We were not going to remain together. We were getting split up into two twosomes. Dresnok and I moved into neighboring houses in a small town called Li Suk in an area outside Pyongyang called Sung-gun-li, while Parrish and Abshier moved to a different town. The cadres claimed Parrish and Abshier were more than one hundred kilometers away (though we would soon discover that they were really only in the next valley over, about a half an hour's walk). This caused an afternoon of confusion as we scrambled to split up the few chickens and rabbits we had been keeping until then. I was sad to see Parrish and Abshier go, but after the four of us had been living on top of each other for so long, having some space to ourselves was a welcome relief.

Actually, we weren't really by ourselves. You are never really alone in North Korea to begin with, but as part of our new living arrangement, the Organization issued us each a North Korean woman as a cook. Each one was supposed to live with one of us to cook, clean, and keep an eye on us. To tell the truth, they were basically supposed to be unofficial wives, fulfilling all of the roles that wives traditionally fulfill. Since they were North Koreans, however, there was never any chance any of us would actually marry any of them, since the Organization would not allow one of its daughters to be the spouse of pigs like us. (Why it was okay for them to be our consorts, however, was yet another contradiction to their twisted logic that I was never able to unravel.) In line with that sentiment, the North Koreans thought that they had ensured there was no chance that we could tarnish the supposed purity of the North Korean race by producing half-breed children. All of the cooks had already been married and divorced by their husbands because they were believed to be infertile. (When Abshier's cook got pregnant in 1978, the Organization must have decided that this policy was not such a good idea, after all, since she disappeared overnight, and within two years, the other cooks had been moved out.)

Lee Sung-ji was my cook. From the very first moment, however, she and I did not get along. Her ex-husband was the police chief of a small town named Hong-ju, south of Pyongyang. He

divorced her at age twenty-eight after years of unsuccessfully trying to have children. The very first thing she said when she arrived at my house and learned the nature of her new assignment
was, "I am not cooking for any American dog. They killed my
father." It mostly went downhill from there. True to her first de-
claration, she hardly cooked at all, which was supposedly her primary reason for being there. And she never cleaned anything.
But more than that, our personalities never meshed. We clashed
all the time.

At first, she tried to blackmail me into buying her things at the
Pyongyang Shop. She threatened to turn me in to the cadres, for
example, for rules that I had broken. I told her, "Go ahead. You
do just as many freedalisms as I do, and I will rat you out worse."
Then she threatened to have sex with Dresnok to make me jeal-
ous. I just laughed at that one. "Go ahead," I told her. "You are
going to have to find something I care about if blackmail is going
to work." So finally she settled on simply bribing me, which
worked a lot better. She had some bee boxes that were producing
a fair amount of honey that she could sell for won, so she had
quite a bit of money coming in. She always wanted me to buy her
things at the Pyongyang Shop, things that locals could not get
their hands on, like nylon sweaters or Seiko watches. I had access
to the Pyongyang Shop but no money. So instead of threatening
me, she gave me a cut of her action, and in return I bought her
some of the stuff she wanted from the foreigners' store.

We found out where Abshier and Parrish lived faster than
anybody counted on. One day, only about a month after we all
split up, Dresnok's cook and mine were out shopping in another
town a few kilometers away when they noticed two houses that
looked exactly like theirs. They went up to the doors, knocked,

and started talking to Abshier's and Parrish's cooks. It didn't take them more than two minutes to put it all together. Later that afternoon, Abshier and Parrish paid us a surprise visit. It had only been a few weeks, so there wasn't much to catch up on. The biggest news was that they both seemed to get along with their cooks, while Dresnok and I were having a hell of a time with ours. That night, we went to check out their houses. (That's what we said, anyway—we really wanted to see how good-looking their cooks were.)

Dresnok turned stoolie on all of us that night and ratted out the fact that we had made contact. He said he got scared that someone would see his shoe tracks in the mud, and since nobody in the whole country had feet as big as he did, they would know instantly he had been somewhere he shouldn't. So he went straight to our leader and confessed. The next day, the Tall Cadre came and bawled us out something fierce. He must have yelled for an hour straight, made us do extra self-criticisms, increased our studies, and didn't let us leave the house. While we pushed the rules as far as we could as often as we could, this infraction really mattered to the Tall Cadre. At one point, he slammed his fist down on a desk and cracked the five-millimeter-thick desktop glass.

I didn't see Parrish and Abshier for another seven years.

Dresnok turning in our visit to Parrish and Abshier was just one of an increasing number of incidents that revealed him as more than ready to become a stooge for the cadres. And September 9, 1972, was a turning point in that regard, a day when he went over the line in betraying me to elevate himself in the eyes of the Organization. Because of what he did that day, and what he continued to do for the next seven years, our relationship probably took twenty years to recover. September 9 was a holiday, the anniversary of the founding of the Workers' Party. So, as on every holiday, we were responsible for entertaining whatever cadres would come over. Once we moved to Li Suk, Dresnok and I would alternate holidays. First he would take one; then I would take one. So, on this holiday, the Tall Cadre was coming over for lunch at Dresnok's. On this day, we were sitting there, just me, him, and Dresnok, in Dresnok's living room, talking about nothing much at all. Another cadre and the driver were waiting outside, and Dresnok's cook was milling about the kitchen, doing her thing.

The topic moved toward sex, and the Tall Cadre started raising hell with me. He said that it had come to his attention that my cook and I were having almost no sex at all. Never mind how he might know this—there are any number of ways—but, more important, this is another example of the control and interest that the Organization can exert over the most personal and private moments of your life. When you are outside the situation, it seems like the most bizarre thing imaginable, but when you are there in the moment, you don't give it a second thought. Even though a cadre is talking about your sex life, it is as if he is talking about something as mundane and customary to discuss as rations or trips into Pyongyang. Anyway, he said that our virtual celibacy was unacceptable (though he didn't say why) and that he was laying down the law. I had to have sex with my cook at least twice a month, he said, or there would be hell to pay. I told him that it wasn't any of his business what I did or didn't do with Lee. But he persisted and persisted, saying he wouldn't let the subject drop until I agreed, which I wouldn't do.

Finally, I just told him to go to hell and to stay out of it. Well, that did it. He practically started to shake, he was so furious. He called the driver over and told him to go to the car and get some rope. He tied my hands behind my back and told Dresnok to beat me for my insolence. I still cannot believe it today, but I'll be damned if Dresnok didn't step right up and do as he was told. He did not even hesitate. And I will never forget the look in his eye. The sick bastard enjoyed it. He took solid, square-knuckled cracks at me across my face, one after another. He must have landed thirty or forty punches in a row, every time looking at the Tall Cadre to see if he should continue. My nose began to gush blood after the first few swings. By the time he had finished, my top lip had split in two places and my bottom teeth were sticking out of the skin between my lower lip and my chin. I still have the scars all around my mouth. I had to struggle to lift my head, but I managed to clear my nose of blood onto the low table we had been sitting at and get up groggily. My only thought was to head out the door to get back to my own home to try to clean myself up and figure out how badly I was hurt. I don't even remember how I got untied. They must have untied me. As I was leaving, I heard the Tall Cadre tell Dresnok's cook to run to my house to tell my cook to hide all the sharp objects, since he was afraid I might come back and kill Dresnok. He hadn't realized that I hadn't left yet. I stumbled back and said to him that he shouldn't worry about me killing Dresnok; he should worry about me killing the person who gave him the order and that he couldn't possibly hide all of the things I was capable of killing him with.

That was the first of approximately thirty similar beatings I received over the next seven years at the hands of Dresnok. For whatever infraction I committed, the Tall Cadre would tell Dresnok to beat me, and Dresnok was only too happy to comply. Why was he always an eager torturer? He had become a stooge. From the very beginning, the North Koreans tried to keep us Americans from becoming too close and always looked for ways to divide us. They encouraged us to tell on each other if one of us broke the rules, promising us rewards or preferential treatment. In exchange, we would get lighter work details, better rations, or an extra trip into town. Of all of us, Dresnok was always the one most willing take advantage of this strategy. Now that we were split up into twosomes, he had clearly decided even more strongly that his best path of self-preservation was to look for ways to elevate himself above me in the Organization's eyes rather than ally with me in a more desperate fight of Us versus Them. And he clearly didn't mind that allying himself with the Organization meant beating me on a regular basis. Decades later, Dresnok stopped being such a stooge, and I managed to put much of my resentment of him past us and forgive him. In the final few years, we even became somewhat close. But for several years, I was surrounded by enemies. The cadres, the cooks, and now even Dresnok.

Perhaps not surprisingly, it was during that time that I began to feel incredible surges of hate that I had never felt before in my life. I would fantasize about driving a knife into someone's heart, anyone's heart, just to see what it would feel like. I would dream of having a gun, especially an automatic, because I had no doubt that if I only had the chance, I could kill tens, if not hundreds, of people. The hate would come in waves and press down on me, like the worst headache I'd ever had or as if someone was sitting on my chest. That's what it was most like, a weight bearing down on me, making me feel like I was being crushed. Sometimes—often, actually—the hate turned inward. The guilt I felt, my inability to try to right the wrongs that I had done, and the living hell that I had landed in—all of it was tearing me up. "How did I get myself into this mess?" I would wonder. "How is it possible I cannot get myself out?" One day around this time, I had had a particularly nasty fight with my cook—about what, I honestly cannot remember. But I had a headache and went to the cabinet where we kept the aspirin. Our doctor at the time was a military doctor, so he prescribed us stuff in bulk, like the amounts that entire army companies would be given. So I opened the cabinet and saw a giant jar of aspirin, perhaps one hundred fifty tablets. Without even thinking about it, I downed them all in enormous handfuls. It didn't take long before my vision started to go all swimmy, and I went to my bedroom to lie down. My only mistake as I tried to kill myself was that I did not take the empty aspirin bottle with me to bed. My cook found the bottle and called the doctor. The next thing I remember is coming around about seven hours later with a doctor hovering over me.

Ultimately, the cook and I made a truce. We simply agreed that we hated each other and were never going to get along, but that we had to live together, so we needed to tolerate each other as best we could. After that, and thanks to the money we were making together, we actually got along okay, and Lee ultimately lasted seven years in my home. They finally shipped her out unexpectedly one Sunday afternoon. No warning, nothing. She wanted to take her honeybees, but they wouldn't let her. I don't even know where she went. I asked the leader the next day if he thought she was ever coming back. He said, "No." And that was that. Looking back at it, I did learn some things from her. She was good at gaming the system. She was good at getting away with stuff and bending whatever advantages she could her direction. She was the one who told me, "Tell the leaders, 'Yes, yes, yes, whatever you say,' to their face, and then when they are gone, do as you please." That was some of the best advice I ever got. After she left, I inherited her bee boxes, so I started a slightly different racket with Dresnok's cook. She would sell my honey at markets I couldn't go to without arousing suspicion, and in return I gave her a cut.

Out of the blue, one of our leaders told us that starting May 1, 1973, we were all going to be teaching English at a military school called Am Ran Gong on the eastern outskirts of Py-ongyang. Apparently, Kim Il-sung had recently visited the school and had noticed that the foreign-language departments had no actual foreigners teaching their native languages, so he declared: "I will find you foreign instructors." So here the cadres were, and with a wave of their hands, a bunch of dropouts were now college instructors. Dresnok and I could really only shake our heads. If we were the best they could do, you know North Korea was pretty hard up for teaching expertise. Our pay got bumped up from ten to twenty won a month.

We all went in rotation. Dresnok and I would go for ten to fifteen days at a time. After we were safely home, they would bring Parrish and Abshier in for a ten-to-fifteen-day stint. The school at that time was a two-year military academy. All of the students were the sons of people high up in the government, and the subjects they studied were primarily foreign languages and military science. At the end of two years, the cadets graduated as lieutenants in the army. We each taught three ninety-minute classes a day. There were about thirty students in each class. There was always one student monitor, who turned on the tape recorder as soon as I began the lesson. The first ten minutes would involve discussing the day's "news" that students had heard over the school loudspeaker that morning. The next twenty minutes would involve going over their homework from the night before. The final hour would be a mix of reading, pronunciation, listening skills, and conversation. Typically, I would have them read from their textbook for fifteen minutes or so. The text usually involved the teachings of Kim Il-sung or the stories of the guerrilla fighters who took on Japanese soldiers during World War II. Then I would ask questions about what they had read, and we would discuss their answers. After classes, afternoons usually involved preparing future lesson plans. All lesson plans had to be approved by the department head, and the only sure criterion I could determine for lesson plans that got approved instantly versus those that got sent back for revision was this: The more often your lesson plan mentions Kim Il-sung, the more likely it is to be approved.

I hated teaching and hated the people running the school. I can't say if I hated my students, since I was never allowed to interact with them outside of class, but I am pretty sure they hated me. With all of the anti-American propaganda they had taken in, some of them would just scowl at me during class, in the hallways, wherever. The administrators tried to keep our interaction with anyone to a bare minimum. When we weren't teaching, Dresnok and I were banished to our dormitory room, which had two beds, two desks, and little else. We took our meals in the officers' mess, but no one spoke to us, and we didn't speak to anyone who wasn't in the English faculty, which had about fourteen teachers besides us. At that school, they taught Chinese, Russian, Japanese, and English. And despite Kim Il-sung's promise to find foreign instructors, we were the only foreign teachers we knew of teaching there besides one Russian woman whom I only laid eyes on once and did not speak to. Wherever some of the Japanese abductees were teaching, I don't think it was here, at least during the years I was there. Obviously, it would be hard to tell a Chinese from a Japanese from a Korean just by looking at him, but one of the other members of the English faculty told me that all of the other languages' teachers were North Koreans who had spent time in the countries of the languages they now taught. I don't know if it's true, but that's what he told me.

Every time I taught, I felt bad that I was helping members of an army that was still the enemy of the United States. But I had long ago learned that large resistances in North Korea were not possible. I could not simply refuse to teach, for example. During those days, if I refused, I knew I would be beaten until I complied (by Dresnok, most likely) or sent to a work camp in the north where death was virtually certain. Small resistances, however? Those were possible. Not that I am an expert in English in the first place, but I purposely took a "Who cares?" attitude to the whole thing. If my students were wrong, sometimes I corrected them, and sometimes I didn't. Occasionally, I would purposely tell them the wrong answer just to see if they would notice. They never did. Very often, a student would say something, and I would have absolutely no idea what the hell he was saying. The last thing I wanted to do was sit there and unravel his gibberish, so I would just say, "Yes, that's right. Very good."

The summer of my first year of teaching, as the weather got warmer, I began to wear short-sleeved shirts to class. This revealed the old tattoo on my left forearm that I got in Killeen, Texas, of two crossed rifles above the words "US Army." Though nobody had noticed the tattoo before, or apparently cared about it if they had, over the previous eight years I had been in North Korea, now that I was in front of young, impressionable cadets, this glorification of Yankee imperialism was completely unacceptable. I didn't know about that, though, until the day they cut it off. One day I was in my room and was called to the school's clinic. When I arrived, a doctor, four or five cadets, and Dresnok were standing there. The doctor looked at my tattoo and squeezed and prodded the skin. He said, "This has got to go. The English faculty said so."

It took me only a second to realize the seriousness of what he was saying, that he was going to hack it off. I told them, "Uh-uh. No way. I am not getting rid of it." He said, "Oh yes you are." He gave a nod, and the cadets grabbed me. They pushed me down onto a stool and held my arm on one of those preacher's benches that are common when you are giving blood or a doctor is working on your hand. They held me down, and the doctor moved in. He cut above and below "US Army" with a scalpel. That part didn't hurt so bad, actually. But when he lifted up the flesh and started cutting all the connecting tissue away with a scissors, that was one of the most excruciating things I had ever felt. I screamed and nearly passed out, gritted my teeth, closed my eyes, and breathed as deliberately as I could. I clenched my jaw hard in a kind of instinctive reaction, I think, to transfer some pain somewhere else.

The doctor told me calmly and without any regret or sorrow at all as he was working that he couldn't give me anything for the pain since they save all the anesthetic and painkillers for the heroes on the battlefield. The cadets holding me down were laughing the whole time, and for weeks afterward they would snicker in class or when they saw me in the hallways. Dresnok, for once, did not seem to be enjoying my suffering as much as usual. He told me later that he knew they were cutting the tattoo off and had come for the show, but he was surprised and even angry when they did it without anesthetic. The doctor sewed the wound up with a needle and thread, and my arm throbbed for days afterward. I didn't even go back to the clinic to get the stitches out. There was no way I was going to let that butcher touch me again. I just let my skin push them out as it healed.

The teaching routine lasted until 1976. On August 18 of that year, some North Korean border guards hacked two American army officers to death in the DMZ with axes as the southern forces were trying to prune a tree that was blocking their line of sight. When that happened, the entire country mobilized for war. All of the students began getting assigned to units that were shipping out of Pyongyang for the countryside. Classes were cancelled, and there was a citywide blackout every night for four nights straight. It was very tense. But for me, there was nothing to do but sit around and wait. Late that same week, on Saturday night, a general came to my room to tell me that they were closing the school for good. A car came at 9:00 A.M. the next day and delivered me home. The war, of course, never came, though the incident is now taught proudly in North Korean schools as a heroic episode in that country's history. While I knew that the North was probably in the wrong about this one, I did not learn until I got out of the country in 2004 just how barbaric and disgusting the North Koreans' massacre had been.

Over the next few years, my job was basically just to study more ideology. My primary task beyond that was translating English-language radio broadcasts from Voice of America, Armed Forces Network, Japan, and NHK's English broadcasts into

Korean for the cadres. This was something I was always happy to do. Not only did it make me feel like I was still a member of the real world to hear normal news, but I also figured that the more that balanced information got out, even to the elites, the better. If it helped convince even one cadre somewhere that his whole country was a lie, then that was a benefit.

Sometime around 1978, Parrish, Abshier, and Dresnok moved to Pyongyang because they were all being set up with foreign wives. Following Abshier's cook accidentally getting pregnant, our leaders told us that the Organization had decided that the policy of providing us female North Korean cooks was not working and that they had found us four Arab women from Lebanon to be our wives. I said no, I wasn't interested, so they left me where I was in Li Suk. Dresnok said he would at least see what the situation was (as did Parrish and Abshier), and he headed out for Pyongyang. I didn't see any of them until about eighteen months after that, but when I did, they filled me in on what happened.

This is what they told me. A Lebanese employment broker working with the North Koreans convinced four young Lebanese women that there were four secretarial jobs paying $1,000 a month in Japan. These four women eagerly signed up. They got on a plane they thought was bound for Tokyo, but really its final destination was Pyongyang. These four were supposed to be our wives. Siham and Haifa were two of their names. The other two I don't know, and I am not sure I ever did. Siham and Parrish paired up, as did Haifa and Dresnok. The North Koreans' plan went wrong quickly for a couple of reasons, however. One of the girls whose names I never learned turned out to be the sister of someone very high up in the Lebanese government or elite society. So right there, those two were gone, back to

Lebanon, never to be heard from again. Siham's mother, meanwhile, who lived in Italy, hired a private detective to track her daughter down. He did a fine job of it, tracking her to North Korea, and now the mother, who also had friends in high places, had some sort of diplomatic pressure bearing down on North Korea. So Siham and Haifa flew back to Italy to Siham's mother. But there was a problem to come for Siham: She got back to Italy to discover that she was pregnant with Parrish's child. So Siham's mother sent her right back to Pyongyang to be Parrish's wife. Because of all her connections, though, Siham enjoyed privileges in North Korea that none of the rest of us even could dream of, almost like she was a diplomat herself. She got to leave the country once ever few years, for example, to visit Lebanon or Italy. She also was able to receive letters and money from home.

In the meantime, the Organization still had to find wives for Abshier and Dresnok. Dresnok's wife wound up being a Romanian woman named Dona. When I first met her in early 1981, she was about twenty-eight years old. According to Dona, she was the daughter of a Russian woman and a Romanian army colonel. Her father molested her throughout her childhood, so she couldn't get out of the house fast enough. When she was in her early twenties, she met and married an Italian and moved to Italy. She got pregnant but had a miscarriage one night after she went out dancing. Dona was doing some hard living—drinking, drugs—that her husband did not approve of, so he ultimately divorced her. With some of the settlement money, Dona went to art school in Italy. She was one hell of an artist. I will give her that. She could draw like she knew what she was doing.

One night, she was in a bar in Italy, and she met an Italian man who asked her about her background, what she was doing in town, things like that. She told him she was an artist, and he asked her if she would like to go on an art tour. He was acting like an art dealer or agent or some sort of big shot but was, in retrospect, a North Korean sympathizer or paid agent. "How about Hong Kong?" he asked her. "There are a lot of interesting things going on in the art business in Hong Kong right now." She didn't have either a Romanian or an Italian passport at this time, for some reason, so he fixed her up with a North Korean one, and off they went. They traveled through Russia, no problem, and they stopped in North Korea before Hong Kong. And in Pyongyang the North Koreans stopped her, claiming her passport was a fake, which obviously it was. But in her panic and under interrogation, they coaxed a confession out of her that she was a spy. And so now they had her, and she wasn't going anywhere. She was stuck there for good.

Abshier wound up marrying a Thai woman named Anocha. The story of Anocha, who was a few years younger than Dona, is far more simple. After growing up in Thailand and becoming a prostitute, she moved to Macau in her late teens to work in a (nonsexual) bathhouse to try to make a better life for herself. One night, on her way home from work, she was jumped in an alley by two men, forced onto a boat, and taken against her will to North Korea. That was just a few months before meeting Parrish. She said there were two more kidnapped Asian women from Macau on her boat on the way over, but she was not allowed to talk to them, and she never saw them again. When the men all returned from Pyongyang with their new wives, Abshier moved in to Dresnok's old house, the one near mine in Li Suk, while Parrish and Dresnok took the two houses in the nearby town.

I am certain that there are many people from many nationalities who have been kidnapped from their own countries or who were tricked into coming to North Korea and are now being held against their will. I saw many people from Hong Kong and Southeast Asia who I am sure had been snatched, and many of the Europeans and Middle Easterners I knew, saw, or met in North Korea were, for one reason or another, unable to leave the country due to obstacles that the North Koreans purposely constructed to keep them there. So ever since arriving in Japan, there is one thing that I have never been able to understand: Why is Japan the only country that is—rightfully—making the return of abducted citizens or citizens who are being held against their will in North Korea a large part of their diplomatic dealings with that country? It is a tragedy, in my opinion, that more countries don't investigate further or take the stand that Japan has, because this should not just be Japan's issue to fight alone. I am certain there are abductees from all over the world in North Korea.

While the other three Americans were off being given their new wives in Pyongyang, I was left alone to deal with my new cook, Go Chung-mi. She arrived less than a week after Lee left, and, no matter how poorly Lee and I got along, it was only after Go arrived that I realized how good I had had it. Go was nicer than Lee, perhaps, but she was impossible to live with because she suffered from seizures. Violent, table-overturning, body-shaking, tongue-biting, rolling-on-the-floor seizures. She suffered from at least one large one and a number of small ones every day. Go's explanation for her condition was that during an operation years ago, they had taken too much blood, and she fell into a coma for three months. When she came out of it, she suffered from these seizures ever since. That explanation didn't explain a whole lot in my book, but at a real level, it didn't matter what the root was. All that mattered was that she couldn't really live a normal life.

Whether the seizures were a symptom or the cause, Go was certifiably crazy, too. She would wear the same apron all the time. I don't mean she was just kind of grubby. She wouldn't take it off for weeks. She would go out and plant or pick corn and then come in and cook, with her hands and clothes still covered in mud. If she spilled a bowl of soup, she would mop it up with the apron and wring it out, then mop up some more and wring it out again, and never change the apron. Sometimes, she would crawl around on the floor, giggling and scrutinizing the floor, looking for flea-sized bugs that weren't there. That didn't stop her from "catching" them, picking them up, and admiring them. I begged the cadres to take her away. I told them that I simply couldn't live like this. Finally, on January 15, 1980, they sent her to a textile mill where they stashed the insane, the retarded, and the socially unfit. I felt bad for her, but she shouldn't have been assigned to be a cook in the first place.

December 1959, before I deserted.

New Year's Day 1975. This was the first time I ever received a gift from Kim Il-sung the way many North Koreans did on major holidays. Inside were three bottles of wine, ten packs of cigarettes, a calendar, a few cans of tinned meats, and assorted cookies and candies. The white card says "Kim Il-sung." The red card says "A gift" and opens to reveal a list of the box's contents.

August 8, 1980, Pyongyang. On the morning of our wedding day, the Organization dragged us around the city for photos in front of a number of landmarks. Hitomi burned all the photos from later that day when she had changed into a traditional Korean dress, but the pictures from the morning photo trip to Pyongyang survive.

Fall 1980, not long after we got married. I remember whenever we posed for photos, it was hard to find a vantage point that didn't have barbed wire.

The family in 1986.

––––––––––

Mika and Brinda in front of the Pyongyang Shop in 1988.
They are wearing the only nice dresses they owned.

On the set of a North Korean movie about the 1968 U.S.S. *Pueblo* incident, 1992. I played the captain of the aircraft carrier U.S.S. *Enterprise*. On the right is another actor known as Dong Chul. They said he was Russian, but I never heard him speak Russian, and I believe he grew up in Korea.

September 2002. Hitomi at the Koryo Hotel in Pyongyang, where she met the Japanese Red Cross for blood tests to prove her identity and received her first official briefing that she might be returning to Japan.

October 15, 2002.

(Above) On the tarmac of the Pyongyang Airport just before Hitomi left for Japan. Megumi Yokota's daughter Kim Hae-gyun is between Mika on the left and Brinda on the right. I am wearing the same tie I wore on my wedding day.

(Below) Pyongyang Airport. I am chatting with Akitaka Saiki, deputy director general of the Japanese Foreign Ministry's Asian and Oceanic Affairs Bureau. At this time, I think he was dropping hints to see if I could be convinced to come to Japan.

April 2004. Before we left North Korea, we had to take photos for our citizenship papers. There was some film left over in the camera, so I took some extra snapshots. This is one I got of James Joseph Dresnok (in the back), Siham Parrish (second from right), and a few of the Dresnok and Parrish children standing with Brinda.

September 11, 2004. This is the day I turned myself in to the U.S. Army at Camp Zama. I walked up to Lt. Col. Paul Nigara, provost marshal of the U.S. Army in Japan, gave him my best salute, and said, "Sir, I am Sgt. Charles Robert Jenkins, and I am reporting for duty" (Corbis).

October 2004, Camp Zama. Awaiting trial.

5 | Soga-san

Soon after Go Chung-mi left, my leaders told me that there would be another woman coming soon. But she was not a cook, and she was not even Korean, though they called her by a Korean name, Min Hae-gyun. They did not tell me she was Japanese at the time, only that she was Asian and that they wanted me to teach her English. Though they first told me about her very soon after Go Chung-mi's departure, her actual arrival did not come until months later. And even on the day she was finally to appear, she was still very late. That's because of the heavy rains that were coming down that made travel nearly impossible. The little bridge closest to my house had washed out, so they had to hook the 280 Mercedes they were driving to a bulldozer and pull it through the thirty-foot-wide river. I found out later that the car had waited six or seven hours for the bulldozer to arrive. Once they were crossing the river, the water came rushing into the car so high that the girl had to pull her feet up onto the seat and perch there like a bird. When they got to the top of the hill, they decided they could not chance driving down the steep, muddy lane that led to my house and chose to walk. But the girl was wearing high heels, so the leader ran ahead to my house to see if they could borrow a pair of my boots. He took a spare pair of leather boots I'd had for years and ran back up the hill to give them to her so she could come down safely.

Finally, on June 30, 1980, at about 10:00 P.M., there was a knock on my door. When I opened the door and Hitomi Soga walked in, my heart stopped. I didn't even notice the driver and the leader she was flanked by. I had never seen anybody so beautiful in my life. Just twenty-one years old, she was wearing a white blouse, a white skirt, and white high-heel shoes. In those grubby, old surroundings, it was like she was from a dream or an entirely different planet.

She walked in and sat down with my leader and her leader. The four of us had a toast, including the always-required words of praise to Kim Il-sung, and we started talking. We were guarded, and it was awkward. She was especially spooked since they did not tell her that she was going to a foreigner's house until she was at the top of the hill. She figured she was going to live with another Japanese woman or at least a Japanese man. And this was North Korea, after all, where you learn early not to trust anyone right off the bat. I didn't know much about the abductees; I had heard only rumors, so I figured even if she were Japanese, which she said within the first few minutes, she could be a true believer. She must have come there by her own choice or her family's choice, to study Juche or something. The leaders left at 11:30 P.M., although I am sure one of them stayed up listening to us. Her Korean was good, a lot better than mine and better even than Dresnok's, who had the best Korean out of all of us Americans. How good her Korean was also made me a little suspicious. At that point, who knew who she could have been? She could have been a spy herself.

That first night we stayed up until 3:00 A.M. talking. Mostly it was small talk about how difficult her trip in the rain had been, where she had traveled from, things like that. As the hours passed and it grew late, I noticed that she was yawning frequently. I asked her if she was tired. She said yes, but she didn't make a move to lie down, even though she was sitting on my bed. I could tell that she was scared that I was going to try to take advantage of her. I tried to reassure her by showing her the extra bedding I had laid down in the corner of the other room. I told her that I would be sleeping in there from now on and that the bed was hers. She must have been exhausted and relieved, because when she heard that, her head hit the pillow, and she was deeply asleep within minutes.

Although I was supposed to be teaching her English, both Hitomi and I knew that the Organization wanted us to get married. A man and a woman didn't get thrown together like that unless marriage was part of the plan. Even though our entire courtship wound up taking only a few weeks, the Organization did not force this marriage like they had routinely forced marriages between foreigners (and North Koreans, for that matter) in the past. I don't know why, exactly, but I imagine it's because they figured there was no way they could make a young, beautiful woman like Hitomi be with a forty-year-old coot like me unless she really wanted to.

They told us to take a few weeks to get to know each other before starting our lessons, and that's what we did. I told the cadres to just leave us alone. To be honest, more than one of the leaders told me to simply claim her as my own. By that, they meant rape her, and usually they used language far more graphic. I told them to go to hell, that I could never do that to anyone, let alone this poor innocent girl. If we were meant to be together, I said, we would wind up that way, and it would be by her choice as much as mine. The worst thing the leaders could do, I told them, was to try to pressure us. For once, finally, the leaders listened to me, and after a while, they kept to the background for the most part.

That first week, Hitomi barely came out of her room. She was very shy. In retrospect, she was probably very scared, too. I didn't have a cook anymore, so while she was at her most shy, I did most of the cooking. One day I would bring her cabbage soup and rice. The next day, I would bring her rice and cabbage soup. "The same thing, every meal!" she soon started to exclaim. It was true. I'm not much of a cook now, and I was even less of one then. Cabbage soup was about all I could make. One thing I did learn to make over the years, though, was kimchi: I can make the best kimchi you have ever eaten.

At the time, one of my regular tasks was to transcribe English-language radio broadcasts into Korean for the cadres, so I had a Korean-made Horse That Leaps 1,000 Ri–brand radio (a ri is a unit of measurement that's about a quarter of a mile) and a tape recorder in my bedroom that I didn't even have to hide. One day that first week, I went into the bedroom and turned on NHK for her. Her eyes got big as headlights, and she started shaking. "You can't do that," she said. "They're gonna kill us! They will cut our heads off!" I said to her that this was my house, and even in North Korea, I would do as I pleased. I told her she could listen to the radio as much as she wanted here. But she never really believed me. She turned the radio off as soon as I walked out of the room, and she never touched it again.

In as many ways as I could think of, I tried to make her as comfortable as possible. I would bring her cider and small sweets when she was studying in her room alone. Another thing I would do was spend a few minutes killing as many mosquitoes as I could in her room before she turned in for the night. The mosquitoes are so big and nasty there, they will practically carry you away. With her permission, I would come into the room after she had turned out the lights. I would sit in the corner with a flashlight pointed toward the floor. Between the light and my scent, many of the mosquitoes that would have been bothering her came over toward me. I would swat as many as I could see for as long as it took, so that she could have a more undisturbed rest. And then I would creep out of the room. Usually, she was already asleep by the time I left.

Soon we started playing cards. Blackjack was the only game I knew how to play well, so we played endless games of blackjack. And we smoked. A lot. In that first month, we must have gone through ninety packs of cigarettes. Other times we played a game that the leaders taught us that was a lot like gin. One time, while we were playing cards alone, I said to her that I had heard that a number of Japanese had been kidnapped and brought here against their will. Without saying a word, she pointed to her nose to indicate: "I am one of them." Before long, she had told me her whole story, which I still cannot believe. It makes me so sad.

On August 12, 1978, Hitomi and her mother, Miyoshi, went shopping at a small grocery shop and general store down the street from their house. They lived in a town called Mano on Sado Island, a small island off the west coast of the biggest of the four main islands of Japan. It is a very beautiful place but very isolated, so much so that in feudal times political prisoners were frequently banished there. For centuries, fishing, farming, and gold mining were the main, if not only, industries. Hitomi, the oldest of two daughters, was studying to be a nurse. On that day, around dusk, the mother and daughter had bought ice cream, among other items, and were walking home. They were just a few hundred yards from home when three men jumped them from behind. That was the last time Hitomi ever saw her mother. To this day, nobody knows what happened to her. (Of course, somebody in North Korea knows, but the government there continues to lie, saying it doesn't know anything about Miyoshi.) I know Hitomi holds out hope that her mother is still alive in North Korea somewhere and that someday they will be reunited.

One of the men wrestled Hitomi to the ground, tied her hands, gagged her, and stuffed her in a black body bag. Hitomi was so stunned and scared that she wasn't even able to scream. The man who grabbed her threw her over his shoulder like a sack of coal and carried her to a small skiff with a motor that was under a bridge spanning a small inlet. The small boat chugged about an hour out to sea, where Hitomi was picked up and carried onto a larger boat and put down in the hold. The next morning, they let her out onto the deck, but there was nothing to see, just an open sea and a virtually empty ship. Whenever another boat appeared on the horizon, they made her go down below again.

They sailed the whole rest of the day and landed in Chongjin, North Korea, on the evening of the thirteenth. The next morning, they gave her breakfast and took her to the beach to look for clams. That is typical of how strange the North Korean cadres are, how out of touch they are with the emotions normal people have. Here they have just kidnapped you and your mother and separated you, they have ripped you from your home street in your own country without any explanation or any idea of what is going to become of you, and they are so out of touch with what they have just put you through and how much you might hate them and fear them at that moment that they see nothing weird in saying, "Now that we have a few moments, maybe it would be fun for you to go to the beach to look for some clams?" They are that crazy. By the end of the morning, a car came to take them to the train station, and Hitomi was on her way to Pyongyang. It was an overnight train. She showed up in Pyongyang at 7:30, the morning of August 15. That day, which marks the end of World War II in the Pacific, is, of course, a holiday in both Japan and Korea, but for very different reasons.

One of the saddest parts of Hitomi's story, in my opinion, is that she and her mother were never considered potential abductees by Japan until North Korea confessed in late 2002 that it had kidnapped her. The announcement by the North Koreans that Hitomi was one of the living abductees took everyone, including the Japanese government, totally by surprise. The Japanese government didn't do anything wrong—I am not saying that. There are too many missing persons to keep track of and too many suspicious disappearances to investigate to think that the Japanese government could be on top of them all. No, the part that makes me sad is the thought of being missing and wanting to be home and yet having no one looking for you. It is like you no longer exist, even though you do.

Hitomi's father was a heavy drinker, so the rumor around Sado was that Hitomi and her mother ran away. For days, townspeople checked all the ferryboat registers and passenger lists on trains on the mainland. Some thought they had committed suicide. I feel very sorry for her father and younger sister, not only because they were left behind like that but also because of the cloud of doubt and the rumors that followed them around for years. Hitomi's father did live long enough to be reunited with his daughter before he died in February of 2005, and that is something to be thankful for.

Here on Sado, where I now live, at least a few times a week I pass by the store where Hitomi and her mother were shopping, the point where they were jumped by the North Koreans, and the bridge under which she was hustled into a boat that whisked her off to sea. And every time I do, I feel an intense sadness for everything my wife has suffered and lost. If fate threw us together, I hope that I have been a good enough husband to at least partially make up for all of the other suffering she has experienced.

After a few weeks of getting thrown in and out of different guesthouses, Hitomi was finally placed with Megumi Yokota. Yokota is the Japanese abductee who was snatched by North Koreans on her way home from badminton practice from her home city of Niigata in late 1977, when she was only thirteen. Today, she is probably the most famous of all the abductees and the strongest symbol for those in Japan working for more information about those still missing. There is much speculation and controversy to this day about whether she is alive or killed herself in the early nineties like the North Koreans say and whether the remains they sent back in 2004 really are hers.

For about eighteen months, Hitomi and Megumi were roommates in a small house in central Pyongyang. Back then, according to my wife, the two girls did little else than study Korean language and Juche philosophy. One of Yokota and Hitomi's early tutors was Sin Guang-su, the notorious North Korean agent who is suspected of abducting at least one other Japanese citizen. Yokota had been in North Korea for a year and her Korean was already excellent, so she helped my wife learn much of her early Korean. Many of the Japanese abductees were forced to teach high-level North Korean spies the finer points of Japanese language and customs so that they could pass as Japanese. That is what Megumi reportedly wound up doing in later years. According to several news reports I have seen since returning to Japan, Megumi spent at least a few years, perhaps through 1988 or after, teaching Japanese to spies. To this day, I am not sure why the North Koreans did not make Hitomi go the route that most of the other Japanese abductees went, and neither is she.

Hitomi says that during the time they spent together, Megumi, who was only fifteen at the time, was horribly homesick and cried a lot. Since they had only each other, it should be no surprise that they became best friends. Years later, we learned that Megumi had named her own daughter Hae-gyun, which was my wife's Korean name. Hae-gyun is a fairly common name in Korea, but I doubt this was a coincidence. I am certain that Megumi named her daughter after her best friend, Hitomi.

Megumi was a badminton player, and she had her gear with her when she was taken. When the girls found out that Hitomi was being moved (to come live with me, it turns out), Megumi gave Hitomi her little badminton bag as a going-away present. It was too small for a badminton racquet, but it held her workout clothes. It was red with the number "17" stitched on the side of it in white, and it had the name "Megumi Yokota" written in kanji characters on the inside in Magic Marker. At one point, we tried to wash the name off, because my wife didn't want a leader to see it, but that Magic Marker was stubborn. So we covered the name with a patch and epoxy. Over the years, I would take the bag to the foreigners' stores as a shopping sack. I would use it to carry sugar or eggs. Then it sat in a closet for the longest time. When I left North Korea in 2004 and was scrambling to collect possessions that were important yet didn't look important (and thus I could get out of the country successfully), I wanted to bring that bag with me as a piece of evidence. Unfortunately, during our final preparations for our trip, I could not get back to the house a final time to collect the bag.

After my wife came to live with me, we were not able to have much contact with Megumi, which I think broke Hitomi's heart. There were only two major points of contact that I can recall, in fact. One time, around 1983 or 1984, my wife was shopping at the Tae Dong Gong Dollar Shop. Back when she and Megumi were roommates, they would go to the Tae Dong Gong Dollar Shop together often, and one of the shopgirls became relatively friendly with them. That night, the same shopgirl was working at one of the counters. Buying things at the Tae Dong Gong Dollar Shop was a complicated process, far more complicated than it needed to be, but here is how it worked. When you saw an item that you wanted, you told the counter girl. She would write you up a ticket and hand it to you. Then you would take your ticket to the cashier and pay. The cashier would stamp the ticket twice and keep half of it. Then you would take the other half back to the counter where you could claim your item.

On this day, I do not know what my wife told the counter girl she wanted—whether it was washing powder, a frying pan, a pair of shoes, or what—but when she did, the shopgirl passed her a folded letter along with the ticket. Hitomi was so surprised and nervous that she just about died. When she was finally home and safe, she unfolded it. It did not begin with a greeting, and the writer did not sign it, but the note started with the characters "GaNaLa," which is the beginning of the Korean alphabet. This would be like starting a letter in English "ABC." "How is the Korean coming?" or something like that was the next line. My wife knew instantly that Yokota had written it. The rest of the note, which was not long, did not offer much in the way of specifics. I am sure Yokota realized how risky sending notes like this was, so she attempted to be vague enough so that her identity would not be revealed if someone else found the note but Hitomi would still know she was okay. The note told my wife that she was doing fine, considering, and that she was living in central Pyongyang. She mentioned that she lived near a large crane that was building the biggest building she had ever seen in her life. My wife and I talked about it and decided that she must be near the gigantic 105-story hotel that has never been finished. Hitomi, after much deliberation and heartache, decided not to send a note back to Megumi through the shopgirl. It was, she concluded, simply too risky to open a regular line of communication this way, no matter how badly she missed Megumi and no matter how tempted she was.

The second time Megumi came into our lives again must have been in 1985 or 1986, since our oldest daughter, Mika, was with us and was about two or three years old at the time. We were shopping at the Rakwon Dollar Store in Pyongyang, and Megumi and a female Korean leader came in. I did not recognize her, of course, but my wife nudged me and said, "That's her. That's Megumi." We were standing in the food section, and

Megumi came up and said hello to me and my wife. I introduced myself, and Megumi bent down and started coo-cooing to Mika, whom I had by the hand but was standing and running around and talking a little at that age. Megumi asked me if I spoke Japanese, and I said I did not, so she began speaking in Korean. "Your wife and I are very good friends," she said. "I know that," I said. "I have heard a lot of nice things about you," I responded. At that point, Mika was pulling on me because a box of cookies had caught her eye. I had a little money in my pocket, so I figured I could afford it, and I was looking for a way to excuse myself so that Megumi and Hitomi could talk privately. I knew what a rare and valuable chance this was for them. I don't know why, but the Korean handler Megumi was with seemed to give her plenty of space, too. So Mika and I went off to buy some cookies, and the two women chatted for no more than ten minutes. After that, as far as I know, we never saw nor heard anything having to do with Megumi until October 15, 2002, the day my wife left North Korea for Tokyo.

Around the second or third week Hitomi and I were together, I started teaching her English. Hitomi knew her ABCs but not much more than that. So we started just with writing, penmanship. But she kept holding the pencil like a calligraphy brush. I would try to correct her form by putting my arm over hers and my writing hand over hers. At first, she was having none of that, flinching at the very touch. But over the next few weeks, as she got more comfortable with me and more comfortable with my instruction, she would let me teach her this way, with my arm and hand moving hers to make the strokes. Not long after that, during a similar lesson, I was teaching her a new word, my hand and arm on hers, my cheek right up close to hers. I turned to look at her, and she turned into me, and we kissed.

I don't know what it was that drove us together. On the face of it, we had very little in common. I do know that we were very lonely in a world where we both were total outsiders. And it took us a very short time to realize that we both hated North Korea. That gave us a strong common bond. One of the leaders, one of the few I ever liked, summed a lot of it up in a conversation he had with me during those early weeks with Hitomi. He said, "You and she don't seem like it, but you are actually the same. You both have nothing here. Together, you would each at least have something." I thought what he said was very true. It wasn't much longer after that that I started asking her to marry me on an almost daily basis. At first, she always said no.

One of those first few weeks after we became a couple, we went to Pyongyang and to the Pyongyang Shop. Now I had been coming here for years, so when the shopgirls saw me walk in with this young, beautiful woman, they could not believe it. Hitomi told me later that she was embarrassed at first and that early on she found it difficult to be with me. Not because I was old or because of how I looked, but because I was a Western man. She had never seen one before me other than on television or in movies. She didn't know how to act around me, and she was self-conscious about what other people thought. In time, as we fell in love and she became more comfortable with me than with anyone else, she simply decided that she didn't care what anyone else thought. That day at the Pyongyang Shop I told her I would buy her anything she wanted. She chose an umbrella, which, considering the rain-soaked day she showed up on my doorstep, was something she needed.

I continued to ask her to marry me, practically every day. But I always did so with total honesty. I told her, "You don't know where they are going to take you next, or when, or what it is going to be like when you get there. If you marry me, then you know that you are going to be able to stay here, and I think you at least like it here, and you know that you are safe. I know that you do not love me. How could you so soon? And I must honestly admit that I do not love you, though I think that I could. And, from what I have seen, I think that you are capable of loving me someday. But we do not have the time and the luxury to have a normal courtship, because anything can happen here, and they could decide tomorrow to take you away."

It wasn't long after that that she said she would marry me. I walked down to the police station. The police station was the only place with a phone, and you had to get permission for every call you made. I rang up the Organization and said, "Come quick, it's an emergency." They came rushing and said, "What is it? What is it? Where is she?" They thought at first that she had run away. I said, "Set a date. Hitomi and I are getting married." They could not believe it. They could not believe that someone like her would agree to marry someone like me. "How did you do it?" they asked. I said it was no big mystery. Number one: I was nice to her and gave her the first of everything. I lit her cigarettes, gave her the best food, made her furniture, and gave her gifts. Number two: I told the cadres to get the hell out of the way so that we could actually get to know each other better. And number three: I told her the truth. I told her that she needed me. I told her that we needed each other, and I assured her that I could protect her.

While it was impossible that we could have developed the deep love that sustains a marriage for decades, there is no doubt that once we decided to get married, we gave in to the emotions of wanting and needing each other. One day, not long before the wedding, we decided to play cards after we had finished dinner. I was out of writing paper, so I ripped the white inside lining out of the pack of Kulak-sae cigarettes I was smoking and told her to make a scorecard out of that. She was hunched over the table, writing on the paper for a minute or two, and then started giggling. "What are you laughing about?" I asked her. "How could there be anything funny about a scorecard?" Still giggling, she got up, turned around, and ran into her bedroom. I unfolded the piece of paper she had left, and it said, in English, "I love you." I got up and went into her room. "Is this true?" I asked. She nodded. I said, "Okay, if you mean it and this is still true in the morning, give me the note again then." I left the note on her bed and shut the door behind me. Usually, Hitomi was never able to move around the house without me waking up. It was small, and for her to get anywhere—to get outside to go to the bathroom, for example—she had to go through my room first. For the first time I knew of, however, she was able to successfully sneak into and out of my room, because when I woke up the next morning, there the note was, sitting on my pillow.

Our wedding was August 8, 1980, just thirty-eight days after we first met. There was no real ceremony to speak of. During the day we went into Pyongyang to have our picture taken, and in the evening we had a celebration dinner at home. The food was nothing special, to be honest. Pig's feet, dumplings, rice, and cabbage. The biggest accomplishment of the day, however, was that with some flour, eggs, and sugar, we managed to improvise a wedding cake. We first took about ten eggs and one and a half cups of sugar, put them in a bowl, and beat them for twenty or thirty minutes until it all began to foam and froth. Then we added one and a half cups of flour, stirring very slowly. We lined a pan with a kind of heavy butcher paper—as usual, we didn't have enough oil to line the pan with—and poured the mixture into the pan. We didn't have an oven, so we set the pan in a boiling pot of water so it floated like a boat. Then we covered the pot and let it cook for about forty minutes. We pulled the pan out, let it cool, and cut and pulled the paper away. It was drier than hell, and there was no icing, but that was our wedding cake.

I had saved up about six or seven hundred won, so I was able to buy a nice bottle of cognac for the wedding. I had some extra money during those days because of the racket Dresnok's old cook and I had worked out. She would sell my honey and chickens at a profit to locals that I was not allowed to associate with, and in return I would give her a cut or buy her stuff at the Pyongyang Shop that she otherwise couldn't get her hands on. I also kept about twenty-five chickens, mostly for the eggs. But as a chicken gets older, its production decreases, so I would sell the older ones. A regular chicken was worth about twenty won, while a big one could go for thirty or forty won. In those days, I also had about three bee boxes that could produce about a hundred pounds of honey per season in the spring and the summer. I could get about twenty won for a half-liter bottle of honey in the summer and three times that much in the winter. At the time, my regular money from the government was only about twenty won a month, so a few bottles of honey a month and a chicken here and there helped out my money supply considerably.

Our leader, chief of staff, an old cook from when we were all in Hua-chun (who did most of the cooking that night), the political commissioner, the political commissioner's aide, and their driver all attended our wedding celebration dinner. My wife wore a traditional Korean dress that night, and she looked radiant. My wife wrote the vows in Korean, and I read them. I wish I could say they were all that romantic or as beautiful as the poetry she now sometimes writes in Japanese, but since this was North Korea, most of it had to be so much party bullshit: how we would live as a family for the greater benefit of the nation, the party, the people, and the Great Leader. We also had to sing a song glorifying Kim Il-sung. At the time, we didn't care it was propaganda. We were just happy to be singing.

We had cheap Korean wine in addition to the cognac. The whole night was filled with toasts, everybody pouring us drinks. Before long everybody was loaded. Hitomi herself was pretty drunk, so I took her into the bedroom to let her get some sleep. The aide said that she needed some coffee, so I got up to go make her coffee. By the time I came back, however, the aide was on the bed with her, his hands on her legs, heading up her dress. I grabbed a heavy metal flashlight and was on him in a flash. My hand was cocked back, ready to lay him out flat, when the driver practically tackled me and stopped me from delivering the punch. There was a lot of commotion and shouting, and the group hustled the aide outside. "Get him the hell out of here," I yelled. I was so mad that I was liable to kill him. Everybody decided that it was time to go, and the wedding party, such as it was, broke up.

Soon after we were married, my wife bought a bottle of sake from the Pyongyang Shop. It was big, and it was the good stuff, so it was very expensive. It was a treat and a treasure to sip that sake, and my wife and I made that bottle last for months and months. Every day or two we would have a little bit, but we savored it, so we would pour each other just the smallest of sips. I loved the pale, cold taste, and to this day, sake is still my favorite drink. Once the sake was gone, I used that bottle to hold cooking gas, and it sat out on the balcony of our apartment for years afterward. I liked having that bottle around because it was an artifact from the days that our marriage had just begun and was a piece of Japan, the homeland that my wife so desperately longed for, here in our house.

I knew how badly my wife missed Japan, and so it wasn't long after we were married that I asked her what the Japanese word for "good night" was. Thereafter, every night before we went to bed, I would kiss her three times and tell her, "Oyasumi." Then she would say back to me, "Good night," in English. It became a ritual from which we never varied. We always wished each other a pleasant night's sleep in the other's native language. We did this so we would never forget who we really were and where we came from. Even though we were in love and thankful to be together, we did this to remind ourselves that this place was not really our home and never would be, and that no matter what happened, she was still Japanese, and I was still American.

It wasn't a month or two after we were married that Hitomi was pregnant. I can't remember the last time I was so happy, certainly no time in North Korea. With a couple more months of getting to know one another, we had learned to trust one another completely and rely on each other absolutely, and with the added excitement of having a child together, we were now truly falling in love with each other.

Things were going so well that of course I was not happy when I was told that I was being moved away from my beautiful, newly pregnant wife for a few weeks to a few months for a new assignment. And what was the assignment? I was being ordered to act in a movie. I remember one time I was watching TV in 1978. All TV in North Korea is propaganda—the worst stuff you have ever seen, but still, it is there, so you watch. It was a movie about the North Korean war (all movies in North Korea are about war, and North Korea always wins), and who popped up on the screen? Parrish, playing the part of a British army officer! I couldn't believe it. It was an early installment of a multipart movie called *Nameless Heroes* that eventually stretched to twenty installments. Well, 1980 had rolled around, and the Organization needed me to play a new part in *Nameless Heroes:* the evil Dr. Kelton, a U.S. warmonger and capitalist based in South Korea whose goal in life was to keep the war going to benefit American arms manufacturers. They shaved my head on top, since my character was supposed to be balding, and I wore heavily caked makeup. I can still remember my first line. I was talking to Claus, the Seoul CIA station chief (played by an Italian vice dean of the music college in Pyongyang), and I yelled: "You coward! You didn't keep the secrets! I will personally telephone the representative of the Federal States, Carl Vinson." (I knew who Carl Vinson was, but what the hell the "Federal States" were, I had no idea. Still, that was the line, so I said it.)

The North Korean movie industry is a joke, of course. The studio, called the Korean Feature Film Studio, was near Manyongdae, by one of my old houses (and Kim Il-sung's ancestral homeland) and about one hour from my current home. Just the fact that they would need us four Americans to act should tell you something about how sorry a state their movie industry was in. Abshier played a CIA agent in Seoul working under Claus. Dresnok was a major in the U.S. Army who owned an aluminum mine in America and thus had a business interest in continuing the war as well. The costumes were often totally ridiculous (the foreign military uniforms, for example, never looked authentic), and they didn't have a lot of sets or props.

In addition, they didn't bring any common sense to planning the filming. For example, they would often film the scenes in the order that they appeared in the script rather than in the order that made shooting most efficient. If, say, there was a scene at Claus's office, then a scene at my office, and then a third scene at Claus's office, they would film it in that order, breaking down Claus's office set and rebuilding it after filming my scene rather than just filming both of Claus's scenes in a row and then filming mine. I knew nothing about how movies were made, but I knew that filming in sequence was not how real filmmakers did it. I actually think that even the North Koreans couldn't have been that stupid. I suspect part of the reason they filmed it that way was because they were often writing the story as they went, all the way up to the day of shooting. There was also such a shortage of foreigners to play the foreign parts that they would draft not just us Americans but also the families of diplomats and whatever foreign businessmen they could find. Throughout the years, all the way up until 2000, I would occasionally be called to the movie studio to play a role in this movie or that. I acted in probably dozens of them. But because they had no money to actually finish most of these movies, I acted in far more of them than ever got made.

In at least two ways, their idea to have us Americans act in the movies backfired. First, the movie sets introduced us to a lot of high-class foreigners from diplomatic circles whom we befriended and who years later would help us get our hands on a lot of black market things like books and movies. And perhaps worse, the movies made me something of a star, or at least a recognizable face, to a lot of North Koreans. After that first movie, sometimes I would be walking down the street and someone would yell, all excited and happy, "Kelton Bac-Sa [Dr. Kelton]! Kelton Bac-Sa!" Regular North Koreans would sometimes ask me for my autograph. For Parrish, it was even more extreme. His character, Lt. Louis London, wound up turning against the British and joining the North Korean cause, so average North Koreans would not just approach him but would treat him like he was a genuine communist hero.

Off and on for the next several months, I was acting in a movie, but I was home on a break during one of the most traumatic experiences of my life and my wife's. When Hitomi was about seven months pregnant, she went shopping and to a doctor's appointment at the Pyongyang Maternity Hospital. The appointment went fine, but on the way back, the road was so bumpy and rutted that she started to bleed. I telephoned the driver to pick her up again, and the next day they took her back to the hospital. They kept her overnight, checked her out, and said she was fine. She got back in the car for the trip back—and the exact same thing happened. She started bleeding, so I called the local doctor. He came by and said he didn't know what to do. So we called the car again the next morning to take her back to the hospital for the third time in four days.

This time, she wasn't fine, and she went into labor that night, two months early. She delivered a son in the very early hours of Sunday, May 10, 1981. A car came unannounced Sunday afternoon to tell me that she had given birth and to get in, because they were taking me to the hospital. When I got there, I went straight to the maternity ward. Our little boy was being held in an incubator. He looked so small and weak. I had never seen such a small human being. He wasn't much over a couple of pounds and not longer than ten inches. I asked the doctors if they thought he would live. They told me if he makes it three days, then he will live, but that it was too early to tell. I had a sense right then that he wasn't going to make it. They asked me not to tell my wife how dire things were, but I knew my wife knew, since she was both a nurse and the mother, and I figured mothers can tell these types of things instinctively.

I went up to my wife's hospital room and told her that her part was over, that she had given birth, and that all there was left to do now was wait. That's when I told her what I had told her many times before during her pregnancy, that she should name our first child. She said that she had decided to name the boy Masahi.

Since spouses are not allowed to stay in hospitals in North Korea, I went home that night. In the morning, a car came to pick up me and Anocha, Abshier's wife, to shop for rations. I thought this was odd, since usually ration day came every two weeks, either on a Tuesday or a Wednesday. But we got ready, and off we went. In Pyongyang, Anocha got out of the car and went into the Pyongyang Shop. That's when the leader told me to hang back, that he had to tell me something. He let me know that the baby had died late the night before, less than twenty-four hours after he was born. I was sad and sorry to have my son die before he'd even had a chance to live, but to be honest, I was more sad and worried for my wife. I went into the Pyongyang Shop and bought her some dried squid, which was one of her favorite foods.

I then went to the hospital, to the hospital chief of staff's office. The chief of staff wanted to know what to do with the baby.

He said the hospital wanted to take care of the body "in the government way," telling me that a baby that was not yet a year old was not yet part of the family. This is the kind of thing that the North Korean government was always doing, reaching into parts of your life in ways that seem perverse and twisted in retrospect. The hospital people never said how, exactly, they would lay the body to rest, and a part of me does not want to know, even to this day. I told them that this was fine, they could do as they saw fit. They also told me not to tell my wife yet that our son was dead, which I agreed not to do. At that moment my wife, who had heard that I was here, came into the office and sat down. There were four or five other people in the room, so I could not have the conversation I wanted to have with her.

That night, I decided to find Parrish and Dresnok and tell them what had happened to my baby. I don't know why. I just wanted them to know. It thought it was important. I also knew that Siham was pregnant at the same time and was expecting soon, and for some reason, I thought it was important that she know what had happened to Hitomi. While we all had seen each other again occasionally over the past year or so, I hadn't seen the others' houses since 1972 when we had gotten in trouble for visiting each other after we first got separated into pairs. I went to the train station nearest them and asked the station master where the two Americans lived. He wouldn't tell me and took me to the police station. The cop on duty wouldn't tell me either, and when he heard why I wanted to see them, he said, "What does it matter to them, your baby dying? Why do they need to know?"

So I left the police station and decided to find them on my own. I walked to where I thought I remembered they were, across the railroad tracks through a farm, and I hit a dirt road that I recognized. Dresnok's house still had its lights on. I went in and told Dresnok. He went to get Parrish. Parrish came over to hear the news. Dresnok and I talked until dawn. It was not because we were connecting on a particularly deep level, to be honest. I was more waiting for the early morning light so I could find my way home. When the sun started coming up, I set out. It took an hour and a half to walk back to my home. As I look back on it, I think that trip to the other Americans' houses was my own odd way of mourning. All alone, I didn't know how else to express my grief.

They kept my wife in the hospital for about ten days. Although our son died on the tenth, they did not tell her until the sixteenth. I think they told her on the sixteenth because they knew that the seventeenth was her birthday. On the eleventh, since I did not know when I would be allowed to return to the hospital, I gave the doctor a brooch to give to my wife for her birthday, which I said was the seventeenth.

Hitomi wrote me a letter after they told her the baby was dead. She told me she was sorry and that she looked at the baby's death as her fault in some way. She said she was sad that she couldn't buy the baby new clothes. I broke down crying when I read that letter, and I cry even now when I think about it. They didn't bring Hitomi back to me until the nineteenth. We were devastated for months afterward, and, in some ways, I don't think you ever quite get over something like that. I am so thankful, though, that we were able to go on and have Mika and Brinda.

Because of my life with Hitomi and the two daughters we have raised together, I never know quite how to respond to the question that a lot of people ask me: "Knowing what you know

now, would you ever cross over to North Korea again?" Everybody who asks me the question wants and expects my answer to be an immediate "No. I would never." But if I did not do what I did, I would not have my wife and my girls, the three most important people in my life. So I always have to disappoint the people asking by saying that I made a mistake and much of the time was horrible, but I can't say that I would be willing to take it all back.

6 | Friends and Strangers

In mid-1981, we all had to go back to teaching at the school where we had taught before. We were still English instructors, but the school had changed. Newly reopened after shutting down hastily in the wake of the Panmunjom incident in 1976, it had become a four-year military college and its name had changed to Mi Dang-hi University. Cadets still graduated as lieutenants, but the school had been enlarged to enroll one thousand to fifteen hundred students and the curriculum expanded to include more subjects. It was now named after an anti-Japanese guerrilla fighter who was captured by the Japanese during World War II. The legendary story that made him a hero went like this: While a prisoner, he realized that he talked in his sleep and that he was inadvertently giving away secrets about the revolutionary movement. His solution: He bit off his own tongue. Every North Korean knows this story.

In addition to our teaching, the school's administrators would frequently give us side work that would often keep us up until almost dawn. Even though the four of us now went for our teaching stints individually instead of in pairs, Dresnok and I had to collaborate on a military dictionary with more than forty thousand words in it, passing off the work to the other as we each left or returned. All the administrators who saw the English typewriter we were using that was part of the college's office equipment would say proudly, "That came from the U.S.S. *Pueblo.*" We had worked on this dictionary during our first years of teaching in the 1970s, and the school still wasn't finished with it. Another time, we wrote an interrogation handbook. It was times like this when I most felt bad about the harm that I could be doing to the United States by helping an enemy country. But on the other hand, I don't know how much harm I was really doing. Mostly we just translated questions into English: "What is your name? What is your unit?" Other than that, we offered very little in the way of sophisticated interrogation advice or techniques, primarily because we didn't know any to begin with. Here is the sort of stuff we would come up with: "If you capture a foreign soldier and there are no translators available, do not beat him up, thinking that that will magically get him to speak Korean. Ask him to write things down, and maybe you will be able to translate whatever information he offers later."

One task that never made me feel like a traitor, though, was translating the soundtracks of Hollywood movies. We had a tape deck that had slow-motion forward and rewind, and we had to capture every word. I assume someone would create subtitles from the Korean scripts we would write. This was not as enjoyable an exercise as it might sound, however. There were no visuals—it was just the sound tape—and they would chop up the tapes into pieces, giving us a few minutes at a time, so we really were just translating strings of words rather than anything that made sense, not enjoying a story. It was hard even to recognize what you were translating. *Kramer vs. Kramer* was one movie I know I did. But with a lot of them, I didn't even catch their titles. There was a movie about the first atomic bomb drop, and another one on an island with a scientist who was growing giant oysters. I did translate a lot of Walt Disney movies, though. Those were easy to recognize. I worked on *Mary Poppins*. I need to see that movie now that I am out and in Japan, because to this day, I cannot tell you what was going on from the parts I was translating. People flying up chimneys? It seemed like some crazy stuff to me, and I could not make any sense of it.

We all taught there for four more years. We hated it there. Everybody was watching us, criticizing us, writing reports on us that would get us hauled before the administrators for dressing-downs and special self-criticism sessions. But none of us gave a shit about being good teachers, so the more we got in trouble, the more we enjoyed secretly sabotaging our classes. We just wouldn't correct the students' mistakes, or we'd purposely teach them nonsense words. So it was a pretty bad combination for everybody. In 1985, we were all finally fired for good when the school at last caught on to the fact that our teaching was actually hurting the students' English more than it was helping.

In 1981, the Organization decided that keeping all of us Americans and our families in different locations was a waste of leaders and other resources, so they decided to consolidate us in a new apartment building. Cadets from the university built it. It was a four-unit apartment building in Li Suk, right next to my old house, which they left standing. (Later, I kept my pig in my old house for a while.) After many construction delays, we finally moved in in late November 1984. For the first time ever, we all were living together with our wives and families in one place. Parrish's and Dresnok's families had the two units downstairs, and Anocha's and my family had the two units upstairs. By Korean standards, these were okay apartments. The front door of each unit opened onto a large hallway, off of which there were two bedrooms, a kitchen, a bathroom, and a living room. This was our house for the next eighteen years straight, until Kim Jong-il revealed in 2002 that Hitomi was one of the living abductees, and our world turned on its head.

You may have noticed above that I said Anocha moved into the other upstairs apartment and did not mention Abshier. That's because before we were able to move in, Abshier died of a heart attack. My wife and I were still living in the house I had had since 1972, and Abshier and Anocha were living together in the other house in Li Suk, the one that had originally been Dresnok's. (Dresnok and Parrish were in the other pair of houses in the nearby town at this time.) Abshier's house and my house were not much more than fifty yards apart.

The day before he died, Abshier was building some shelves. I had to come and help him. He was hard working but not handy, and it was rare that he ever actually finished anything. If I hadn't come over, he would have abandoned the job. He was funny in a lot of ways like that. He was just not very practical. For example, his conversational Korean was not very good, but he would spend hours studying the newspaper, looking for the hardest words to master, economic and political words. He loved doing that, but he would have been better off learning to speak to the leaders and farmers better. But no, he was happiest when he could slide a word into the conversation that Dresnok didn't know.

That night, Abshier had dinner with Anocha as usual. It was Sunday night, so there was "international time" and a Chinese movie on TV. He was nodding off throughout the whole movie, which was odd for him, Anocha said. Around midnight, he said his chest felt very tight, and he got up to go to the bathroom. As soon as he reached it, he collapsed. Years ago, I had installed an alarm system, which was really just two bells, like small school bells, that connected the two houses. If you pressed the button in one house, the bell would ring in the other house, to alert the other family that something was wrong. Anocha went running for the alarm and pushed it and pushed it, but nothing happened. I had told Abshier and Anocha a couple of days before that since we had just had Mika, we were going to disable ours, but Anocha forgot. After a few moments of nothing happening, Anocha came running and pounded on our door. I went running back over to Abshier's house. There I found him sprawled on his back on the bathroom floor. I will never forget the look on his face as he looked up at me, his eyes rolled back, as I stood behind him. He was trying to say something, but all he could do was groan and then exhale heavily. I knew that was his last breath.

I ran out to the security agency station to get a doctor. By the time the doctor got there, it was about an hour later, and we had dragged Abshier to his bed. The doctor's pronouncing him dead was just a formality. He died just after midnight on the morning of Monday, July 11, 1983. The funeral was the next day, Tuesday, in his house. Since he was a teacher at the university, he had a somewhat fancy funeral, though for nonparty members, that is still not saying a whole lot. His body was placed in a simple wood box, but it was draped with a red cloth. Next to his coffin was a photo of him and the medal he received for appearing in films. (You had to appear in two installments of *Nameless Heroes* to get a medal. At that time, I had appeared only in chapter 20, so no medal for me. Actually, I never got a medal.) A general and a colonel from the school came, and they gave Anocha five hundred won. There was lots to eat and drink. Abshier was buried about two miles away from his home. His headstone said he died on July 10. It also said he was born in Pyongyang. I told the cadres that the date was a mistake and that the birthplace was simply ridiculous. They couldn't have cared less about either one of those things. I knew they wouldn't, but I thought I owed it to Abshier's memory to at least point it out to someone. His grave is about half a mile from the hospital where Megumi Yokota supposedly committed suicide. If we were in North Korea now, I could take you straight to both places.

Abshier and Anocha did not have any children, so Anocha, over the next several years, played the role of aunt to the rest of our growing families. Parrish and Siham had three sons. Nahi was the first of all the kids (and the baby that brought on Siham's return to North Korea after she was freed by her mother's efforts). He was born in April 1980. After that, Siham had Michael in August 1981 and Ricky in the spring of 1986. Dresnok and Dona had two sons. Ricardo was born in late 1980, and Gabi was born in the spring of 1984.

As for Hitomi and me, Mika was born June 1, 1983, and Brinda came along July 23, 1985. The births of my daughters were two of the happiest days of my life. Because we lost our son, it was still my wife's turn to name our first child. She chose Mika, which means "beautiful," and the middle name of "Roberta," after me. The second child's name was my turn. I chose Brenda Carol, which was the name of my half-sister back home. I chose that name because I wanted my daughter's name to be a continuation of my family back in the States, but I didn't want to hurt the feelings of any of my other five sisters. Since Brenda was the last child and the only half-sister, she was special in a couple of ways, so it was easy to choose her individually yet also have the name be a way to pay tribute to the whole family. About the discrepancy between the spellings of my sister's and my daughter's names—how my daughter became "Brinda," spelled with an "I" instead of with an "E," the way my sister spells it—I can't really say, except that until two or three years ago, nobody ever wrote my daughter's name in English. Somewhere along the way, whether it was a transcription variation between English and Korean or just a mistake that someone made once that then kept getting passed along, the spelling got changed. Now my daughter is "Brinda," and "Brinda" she will remain.

Even as our apartment building seemed like one giant nursery and all of the children were great playmates, it would be a stretch to say all the adults got along well. It wasn't long after they met, for example, that Dona started in on my wife. Dona's favorite way to torment Hitomi: to try to convince everyone that Hitomi was actually a Korean and a spy sent to nail us all. She would tell anyone who would listen that she suspected Hitomi's story about being Japanese and being kidnapped was all a big lie. One of Dona's favorite points of proof? Our wedding pictures, in which Hitomi was wearing a traditional Korean dress.

I came home from teaching at the university one week to find my wife crying hysterically on the bed. I asked her what the matter was, and she said, "I have done something horrible." I asked what she did, and she said, "Something awful." So I asked her again, and she responded, "Do you promise you'll forgive me?" At this point, I began to fear the worst, that she had cheated on me or murdered someone or something like that, so I got panicked and became impatient. "Dammit, woman, what did you do?" I yelled. At which point she sobbed, "I burned the wedding pictures!" Jesus, what a relief! I was sorry to see the wedding pictures go, but after that buildup, I can honestly say I was happy to hear that that was all it was.

It was around this time that Parrish supplanted Dresnok as the biggest stooge for the North Koreans. Since his wife was allowed to go back and forth to Italy to see her mother for a few weeks every few years, and since they received money from abroad, he thought he and his family were better than the rest of us. Siham, too. She cultivated such a superiority complex that the rest of us started sarcastically calling her the "Imim-bong jang," which is a party designation for someone under a leader who is the boss in charge of watching a floor or a set of floors of an apartment building.

Even with the frequent personality clashes that occurred among such a small group in these strange and often stressful circumstances, we all realized that we had no choice: Our four families had to try to get along the best we could. We had to, since we were forced to do everything together. Take our children's education. After we moved into the apartment, the house that Abshier and Anocha had been living in was turned into a kindergarten, just for our kids. (That house was also the leaders' quarters.) There were three little desks in the house's main room, and each of our kids would spend two years there, from about the time they were six until they were eight. Nahi, Ricardo, and

Michael were the first "class." Mika and Gabi were in the second "class." And Brinda and Ricky were in the third "class." There, they would learn to count, recite their alphabet, and, of course, learn their first revolutionary songs singing the praises of Kim Il-sung and Kim Jong-il.

Once each "class" got out of kindergarten, the children enrolled in the school that was part of the large collective farm that bordered our house. The schoolhouse itself was about a thirty- or forty-minute walk away, and the school had about thirty or forty students per class. The farm school had a grade school, a middle school, and a high school. I was not much of a student myself, so I am not one to judge, but it didn't seem like the schools taught much more than propaganda. They watched movies and got lectures almost constantly about how evil Americans were. Surprisingly, however, none of our kids experienced discrimination at school because they were half-American. They were treated more like exotic and rare specimens rather than half-breeds or mongrels, as you might have guessed. Even so, I tried to tell my girls not to believe all of the America-hating stuff they were taught. For some reason, Mika seemed to buy into the propaganda a bit more than Brinda did, but one of the many reasons I am glad Mika and Brinda are out of North Korea is that they can finally get a proper education. You spend that much time on indoctrination, I figure, and a lot of the reading, writing, and arithmetic just had to be neglected.

Aside from the propaganda, there were other ways in which North Korean schools were unique. How many other countries do you know of where the students have to pull guard duty to defend their school from thieves—and the primary class of thieves they are guarding against is the army? Girls and younger boys only pulled daytime duty, but older boys would be required to guard at night throughout the week and over the weekends. As they would anywhere else in North Korea, soldiers would steal anything they could get their hands on, but what they wanted most of all from the school was the preserving alcohol used during science experiments. They didn't want to drink it, and they certainly weren't dissecting frogs. The army wanted the alcohol to put into the radiators of the their tractors, since they didn't have any proper antifreeze.

The 1980s were probably the high point for sighting abductees and other noteworthy foreigners. There were always foreign diplomats, exchange students, and a few businessmen and NGO workers in Pyongyang whenever you went. But I am talking about Japanese and people of other nationalities who you could just sense were there for mysterious purposes. I don't know why our contact with them dropped off dramatically in the 1990s, but my theory is that it had something to do with the aftermath of Korean Airlines Flight 858 getting blown out of the sky in late 1987 and the female North Korean agent who confessed a lot about the Japanese abductees' involvement in spy training. The Organization must have clamped down on them after that. Our conduct didn't change in the 1990s, after all. We still kept going to the same hotels, shops, and hospitals in Pyongyang, but we simply bumped into fewer people like that, the ones you would see and say to yourself, "They have a story North Korea would prefer we didn't know."

For example, one day in 1986, Parrish, Siham, Hitomi, and I were shopping at the Rakwon Dollar Store. It's a two-story building, and we were at the top of the main staircase when Siham nudged Parrish and Parrish nudged me. Two non-Korean Asians were coming up the stairs. Parrish said, "That's the Japanese we were telling you about." It was a Japanese man and his Japanese wife. "Good afternoon," said the Japanese man. "How are you?" he asked, in some of the best English I had heard from a nonnative English speaker in all my time in North Korea. The man was very handsome. The woman was also good looking, though her very thick glasses made that harder to see at first glance. The woman and Siham obviously knew each other from before and exchanged greetings. The man and the woman did not seem to be with a leader, though neither were we at the moment, and we chatted in English for about five or ten minutes. At the top of the stairs was a counter filled with pens, stationery, and small office equipment. The couple was looking for a tape recorder, and as the man did most of the talking, the woman examined the tape recorders under the glass very intently. They took a good, long look at my wife as we talked, but Hitomi hung back and did not reveal herself to be Japanese.

Not less than a month before, Siham had returned from the hospital after giving birth to her son, Ricky. She said that her roommate in the hospital was a Japanese woman who had had a son about a week before. During their time together, Siham told us, the woman said that she and her husband had been kidnapped from Europe where they were studying English. She also said that the woman told her that the people who took them were members of the same Japanese terrorist organization that had hijacked a plane in 1970.

After returning from North Korea, my wife and I realized that Siham's story and our memories of the Japanese couple's appearances matched Toru Ishioka and Keiko Arimoto exactly. Ishioka and Arimoto were both kidnapped from Europe—in

1980 and 1983, respectively—by Japanese people who were affiliated with the Red Army Faction members that in 1970 hijacked to Pyongyang Japan Airlines Flight 351, a plane known as the *Yodogo*. During the 1970s and early 1980s, the Japanese Red Army faction was one of the most notorious radical, paramilitary groups in the world. Ishioka and Arimoto are the couple that the North Korean government says died on November 4, 1988, of carbon monoxide poisoning from a faulty home heating system. The North Korean government also claims that the couple's child, who they say died on November 4 as well, was a daughter. But I am absolutely certain that Siham said that the woman had had a son.

There was another Japanese woman whom we saw seemingly everywhere between the years 1980 and 1985. She was short, very pretty, and in her early twenties. She was always alone, except for being accompanied by a leader and a driver. We saw her oodles of times at the Rakwon Dollar Store. We saw her several times a year, but we could never time it just right to speak to her. The last I heard of her was in June of 1985. I was in the hospital at the time since I had broken my collarbone. Parrish, Siham, Anocha, Hitomi (who was about eight months pregnant with Brinda), Mika, Nahi, and Michael were all on their way to an amusement park at Manyongdae and stopped by to see if the doctor would let me come with them. But the doctor said no way. Parrish told me later that they had all spotted the Japanese woman at the amusement park. When you walk into the park, on the left there is an arcade, with things like an electronic shooting range and a game where you hit the heads of the plastic gophers that pop out of holes. She was in there, Parrish said, completely alone, and there were a couple of Koreans guarding the door. They told him he couldn't go in there, but he told them to go to hell. He pushed his way through and was about to say something to her, but she took the commotion as a sign to skedaddle before he could. As the rest of his group came in the door to the arcade, she and her Korean minders were on their way out.

In 1982, Hitomi, Anocha, and I went to a musical at the Mansudae Art Theater. *The Song of Paradise* was the name of the show. We were in a box seat along the side on an upper balcony. In the box seat next to ours were two young Japanese women. We could not see them because there were dividers between the boxes, but we could hear them speaking Japanese. I tried to mess with them by saying the only Japanese words I knew as loudly as I could. I would go, cough, cough, "Arigato!" over the divider. My wife, who was sitting next to me, would secretly pinch me hard to get me to shut up. When the show was over, we dallied as long as we could on the street to catch a glimpse of them. Eventually, they did come out. We saw them get into their car with their leader and drive off. Japanese were not the only abductees, of course. Dona, Anocha, and, to a lesser extent, Siham were all abductees, after all. We never met any other people who confessed to being stolen from their homelands, but over the years we would learn to spot people we suspected were not there by choice. The way they looked, the types of leaders they were with, the cars they were chauffeured in—you just learned to develop a hunch for these things. I have looked at all the pictures of suspected female Japanese abductees, and none of them looked like the two women in the theater or the woman we used to see frequently in Pyongyang. I cannot guarantee I would be able to recognize them again like I could Ishioka and Arimoto, but so far I haven't seen any other photos of people who look familiar.

Americans were a real rarity in North Korea. Some of them would come in for diplomatic meetings or NGO work, I suppose, but I never met any of them. The only people I was 100 percent certain were American were our foursome. And there was Suhr Anna. I am sure about her, too. I am not sure the whole history I heard about her is true, but I am sure she was American. She was a legendary (or maybe "notorious" is the right word) person in North Korea. The supposed backstory on her was that her husband was a radio broadcaster in Seoul when the war broke out. His radio show made a broadcast railing against the war, and the South Korean Army came and shot him, but she escaped to the North. Once set up in the North, they say, she became Seoul City Sue, the Tokyo Rose figure who made English-language radio broadcasts during the war trying to break the morale of American soldiers in the South by telling them how their girlfriends back home were probably cheating on them or just by reading the names of American soldiers who had been killed that day. I don't know if anybody has been able to answer the question of whether she was a true believer or a kind of abductee or prisoner herself who was forced to help North Korea against her will.

Later, she became in charge of all English publications for the Korean Central News Agency. Abshier had dinner with her once, in 1962, just after he had crossed over. That dinner was part of a photo spread for a propaganda pamphlet called "Lucky Boy." There was a picture of them in that pamphlet just laughing their heads off like they were having the best time in the world. Abshier said Suhr Anna told him that it was hard at first to live in North Korea but that he would eventually come to like it.

I met her in 1965 when I went to the "foreigners only" section of the No. 2 Department Store. I was by myself. (Our leader at the time had just said, "Yeah, go on; go ahead," when I asked to go to the store and let me go alone.) I recognized her from the "Lucky Boy" pamphlet, so I walked up to her and said, "Hello, Suhr Anna-senseng" (*senseng* is the Korean word for "teacher"). It was winter, and she was wearing a black leather overcoat, very put-together. She looked surprised and turned, looked at me, and said, "Oh, you must be the American who just came over." I said, "Uh-huh," but she was spooked. The second we met, she wanted to get the hell out of there. She excused herself, saying she really needed to be going, and was gone.

That was the last I heard of her until 1973. We were teaching at the military school, and one of the instructors said he was going to the Korean Central News Agency to pick up some texts or booklets or something. Dresnok said, "Say hello to Suhr Anna for us!" The teacher dropped his things and said, "You want me to say hello to that dead, goddamn spy!?" We had no idea what he was talking about. He told us that they caught her in 1969 as a double agent. She had been secretly feeding information to the South for years, he said, and they executed her. I have no idea if any of this is true, but that is what they told me, and we certainly never saw her again or heard from anyone who had.

People always ask me about Joseph White, the U.S. Army private who walked across the DMZ in 1982, the first GI to do so since I did. But I never met White and never saw him, except for watching the press conference he did in Pyongyang shortly after he crossed on TV. He was wearing his uniform and gave some predictable words of praise to Kim Il-sung and the paradise he had created in North Korea. Watching White, I considered my-self lucky that I never had to do one of those press conferences. I never heard from him or saw him again. On April 15, 1984, though, we were having a holiday party, as always, for the cadres (April 15 is Kim Il-sung's birthday), and I said to one of them, "Why don't you bring White here? We could use another face, and if they got along, he could be Anocha's new husband." (As early as 1972, the Tall Cadre had told us that we were such a bunch of fuck-ups that they would never, ever put any more Americans with us, so I knew this was a long shot.) But this cadre—a guy we called the One-Hour Cadre since he never overstayed his welcome, unlike all the others—just said, "Uh-uh. We can't use White." He said that White had had some sort of accident or stroke and was now paralyzed. And that was the end of that. I have found out since getting to Japan that the most often told story about White was that he drowned around 1985. I don't know which story about him is true. Maybe both. Maybe neither.

Anocha left in April 1989. A few months before her depar-ture, some cadres came to say that they had found her another husband. She wanted to stay and have the husband come here. And we wanted that, too. The Organization said that would not happen. Her new husband was a German and did some sort of business that required frequent trips abroad, so maybe it wound up being a big step up for Anocha. Regardless, we were sad to see her go because she was the person in the apartment building we were closest to by far. Hitomi was particularly sad because they had become very good friends over the years. The night before Anocha left, she came over to our apartment for a farewell party. It was just the three of us. She brought a bottle of wine and a cassette tape of American rock and roll songs from the 1950s and 1960s. We got drunk and did the twist all night long, playing "Tutti Frutti" by Little Richard over and over and over again.

Most of our contact with foreigners was with people whose presence there could easily be explained—students, diplomats, businessmen. I know the Organization preferred we didn't associate with them, but as long as we did it in limited doses, there wasn't much they could do to stop it. A lot of Syrians were studying medicine at the No. 11 Hospital, which was right near the Pyongyang Shop, for example, so we would see them often and got to know some of them pretty well. Siham would speak Arabic with them, and she would frequently trade foreign currency with them. She would trade money with them on our behalf, too, saying she got a better rate because they were more comfortable dealing with her, but she always took a monstrous cut. Through acting in the movies, I also became friends with people like the son of the Cuban ambassador. And through a chance meeting in the Pyongyang Shop, I became buddies with the Nigerian ambassador, too.

One big character in our lives was an Ethiopian named Sammy who was a composition student at the Pyongyang music college. Sammy would hang around the Pyongyang Shop's restaurant every afternoon. He was there so often, it was like his home. I doubt he ever studied. He was the person who slipped us most of the movies we would watch. In 1989, Parrish bought a VCR for about 620 won. Having a VCR was legal, but the biggest problem was that there was nothing to watch. We told Sammy we were sick of watching North Korean propaganda movies on tape, and he said he would start bringing us real movies.

We soon developed a handoff system. Whenever we went to the Pyongyang Shop's restaurant, we would take a bag with us.

Sammy, as I said, was almost always guaranteed to be there. As you walked in the restaurant, there was a window to the left that had long, floor-length curtains. Behind these curtains was the drop-off point. After we walked in, Sammy would get up, disappear for a few minutes, come back, and sit down at our table. While we were chatting, he would mention that "things were in position." That was our signal that the tapes were there and the coast was clear. One of us would get up and grab the tapes he had just left there.

Thanks to Sammy, we got to see a pretty steady supply of Western movies. We would watch them at Parrish's house, with all the curtains drawn and the volume turned down as low as possible. That was how we became familiar with Michael Jackson's music. Sammy brought us "Thriller" on video. I have to say, Michael Jackson seemed like a pretty strange guy even then. Some of the many movies he lent us included a lot of the James Bond movies, *Titanic, Cliffhanger, Coming to America,* and many of the *Die Hard*s. Sometimes it seemed like there were as many *Die Hard* movies as James Bond movies. For a few years in the early 1990s, Parrish got into the black market tape-selling business. He got a second VCR and would duplicate the tapes he borrowed from Sammy, cramming about four movies onto one cassette at LP speed, and then he would give them to his son, Michael, to sell to some Chinese he knew in a nearby town.

My daughters didn't watch the movies much. I think it was hard for them to relate to them. They seemed so strange and otherworldly; they could hardly make sense of them. In *Coming to America,* for example, Eddie Murphy stars as an African prince who finds a wife in New York City, but Brinda and Mika had always been taught that black people in America were still basically slaves, so to see these shots of all the races walking around freely and basically getting along with each other on the streets of New York City was too much for them. Even though *Coming to America* was a fairy tale involving princes and princesses, I tried to tell them that it was still a better view of what the world was really like than the life we were living. I would always tell them, "We are not in the real world. This is not the real world." But they didn't believe me. It was the only world they knew.

7 | Domestic Life

I am well aware that we Americans and our families were a special, even privileged group in North Korea and that our tales of hardship do not compare to the truly unimaginable suffering that so many North Koreans endure every day. Perhaps millions of North Koreans have already starved to death since famines began hitting the country in the mid-1990s, and a huge percentage of the country's citizens still live with the constant torture of not having enough food to eat or clean water to drink. In addition, many hundreds of thousands, if not more, have been worked to death and are still being worked to death in the nation's prisons and gulags. Our situation, it is true, was never remotely that dire. We always had a shelter and never went without food for more than a day or two. But even so, the life we lived was never easy, and our "privileged" existence here would have been considered unspeakable in much of the rest of the world. Our battles with cold, hunger, thirst, poverty, and inadequate sanitation were constant, day in and day out, year in and year out.

I can begin with the cold, since that is the thing that I can still feel deep down in my bones. Our apartment building had a heating system, but it was a good day when we actually had adequate heat. Our house used a hot-water system fired by a coal-burning boiler that sat in the basement. We were responsible for tending to our own boiler. At first, we split the job up. Every year we would start the fire in October or November. Parrish, Dresnok, and I would then each take ten days per month until we shut it down, usually in March. Parrish developed some health problems, mostly involving his kidneys, in 1986, and he bowed out. Then Dresnok came down with heart trouble in the early 1990s, so that left it to me to keep the apartment warm.

Every year we got about twenty tons of coal for the winter. Some trucks would usually bring it in several big shipments over a couple of days in September. We had a storage room in the basement to keep the coal dry, but the leaders would sneak in and help themselves, chipping away at our supply. The first step when you get a coal delivery is to sift the rocks out of it and put it in storage. Then, you can't just shovel the coal straight into the furnace. You need to make it more stable and slower burning by mixing it with clay. We had a huge mound of clay outside, which we used to make this mixture: We blended three shovels full of coal with one shovel of clay, stirred it with water, and formed it into a mound or brick. But the clay-and-coal bricks need to be dry, so it is best to build them well in advance. It is important to always have enough on hand, because if the fire goes out, it takes at least half a day to build a good, hot boiler fire from scratch. And you can't let an extinguished fire set for more than a couple of hours because not only will you get cold, but the water will freeze and the pipes will burst, and then, brother, you really have problems.

The pipes were crooked, so half of the building was never properly heated. And sometimes, because of bad construction, air pockets would form in a pipe somewhere and water would get stuck, so you'd have to boil the hell out of the tank to just force the water through the system. Or you'd have to plunge an outlet valve to get things moving again. If you take care of the boiler like you should, you really should be there all day, stoking the fire and tending to it. But in practice, I would load and stoke it three times a day: once at dawn, once around lunch, and once before I went to bed. Three times a day, I would go right up into that fire. I'd come out covered in soot, blacker than night. That's why I kept a separate set of clothes outside. I would change into and out of them just to stoke the fire, so I didn't track soot into the house too badly. But washing up three times a day, scrubbing coal off of your face without hot water? Now that's a chore. Finally, around 1997, I got one of the leaders to agree that I needed some help, so after that, I usually had an Organization flunky on rotation with me.

Even with all of my best efforts, the apartment was still colder than hell. The bathrooms, hallways, and kitchens were not piped for heat at all, so the warmest parts of the house could get up to sixty degrees on good days, while other parts would plunge well below freezing. Cooking oil and soy sauce freezing in the closet was a regular winter occurrence. We would routinely walk around and sleep in four or five layers of clothes. I remember one time I had a cold, so I went to bed with a couple of aspirin and a glass of water. I put the water on my nightstand, and it froze right there in the glass overnight.

Because it was the furthest away from the boiler and on the windiest corner, Mika and Brinda's room was also one of the coldest rooms in the apartment building. To help them in the cold winters, I improvised an electrical floor heating system. I took four hundred yards of 0.7 millimeter copper-insulated wire and laid it down on the cement floor of their room in a back-and-forth, back-and-forth pattern. Then I covered over that with another layer of thin cement. I hid a flip switch behind their wardrobe. It threw some pretty good heat, even though the current rarely ran at the 220 volts it was supposed to. And this heating system only worked when we had electricity, which was pretty rare.

I would say that before 1997 we had electricity about half the time through the summer and very rarely during the winter. After 1997, we had electricity during the summer only sporadically and almost never during the winter. In the final few years, we had almost no electricity at all, except on major holidays. For example, we could usually count on a couple of days of steady electricity around Kim Jong-il's birthday on February 16. During long stretches, when we had no continuous power, perhaps twice a week we would get an hour or two of electricity. When that happened, we would focus our energies on pumping water into the house. Back in 1978 and 1979, I had dug the well myself—30 feet deep, 7.5 feet long, and 7.5 feet wide. It was about a hundred yards away from the apartment building, and we had to pump the water up to a holding tank on a hill about a hundred yards past the apartment building.

We had an electric motor to pump the well. It was a fourteen-kilowatt motor, but we really needed a twenty-one-kilowatt one to do the job, so even when the electricity was working, it was so weak that the water would rarely get to the tank even on the best days. So usually, we pumped water straight to the apartment building. But even then, it would usually only get as far as Parrish's and Dresnok's places on the first floor. So my family and Anocha would have to carry our water up from their houses in buckets. We had a twenty-gallon tank and a fifteen-gallon tank in the kitchen and another fifteen-gallon tank in the bathroom. Brinda and Mika have probably carried more buckets of water up a flight of stairs than they could count.

After that, we would have to boil every ounce of water we had for drinking. In North Korea, lots of people suffer from intestinal problems from drinking untreated water. Between boiling water for drinking and cooking food, that left very little gas for heating water for our baths. We had a bathtub that I bought from a supply man for 335 packs of cigarettes, but the fuel was simply too valuable to waste on bathing water. We did our cooking with gas, which came in four-gallon cans that we would refill at the hardware store. The cans themselves were hard to get, and gas was scarce. More than a few times we took our can in to get refilled and some bigwig cadre or someone from an embassy showed up and raised a fuss. The people at the hardware store simply gave them our gas and our can. And that was that. There was nothing you could do about it, except to give them a good cussing until you felt better and start trying to work angles to get yourself a new can. When we didn't have gas, we would go outside and build a wood fire to boil our water. Everyone in my family can probably count on one hand the number of hot baths they took at home in North Korea. It is the reason that going to the public bathhouse in Pyongyang once a week was such a treat.

Then there were the toilets. In the winter, since we never had the electricity to fill the main water tank on the hill and thus never had running water, we would have to dump a bucket of water into the bowl to flush the toilet. And the take-away pipes of the toilets were so small, they would frequently clog up. It would be a stretch to say we had a septic tank. Our sewage ran raw onto the open ground about forty yards away from our house and down a hill. Rats would frequently come up the pipes. A live rat once came up through Siham's toilet. She chased that thing around the bathroom with the nearest pipe or club she could find—maybe it was a plunger—but the rat ran right back down the toilet. Once every few years a rat would die in the plumbing, so I would have to go up into the plumbing system and fish out the rat that was plugging up the whole works.

Since electricity was scarce everywhere, candles were one of the hardest things to get in the whole country, even in the foreigners' shops. But that didn't matter, since North Korean candles were total crap anyway. It was better to make your own. At the hardware store, you could usually get paraffin, so I would buy it in one- or two-kilo blocks. Then I would break it up into chunks and put it in a teapot to melt it. I would also throw in the stubs of crayons I would tell the girls to save from school. That gave it a little color. Once the paraffin was melted, I would pour it into a plastic pipe about eight or ten inches tall that was stopped up on one end with a soda bottle top (which fit its circumference exactly). I had already made a hole in the soda top and knotted some cotton string (other fibers won't work) on the outside and run the string up through the inside of the pipe and out the other end. At the top end, I would hold the string taut with a hairpin while also lining it up to make sure the string didn't touch the edges. Then I would dip the pipe into a coffee can of cold water to speed its hardening. With five or six pipes working at once, I could make about one hundred candles a day. Try as I did, I could never find exactly the right cotton string, the kind that dis-integrated as it burned. All the string I could ever find would char but not evaporate as it burned, so unless you kept your eye on the wick, it would grow long, droop, hit the outside edge of the candle, melt it, and cause it to fall over. That's why every night I had to patrol the house a few times, tugging the tops off of the burnt wicks with tweezers.

Since we rarely had any electricity, we had a hand-cranked generator for our television, a black-and-white Chinese portable I bought for $31. Later, we could run it off of a twelve-volt battery I bought. The battery was rechargeable off of house current (which rarely mattered since the whole reason we had the battery in the first place was because the house current never worked) or by using a gasoline-powered generator I had outside. Gasoline, however, was even harder to come by than cooking gas, so we usually made do with the hand crank.

Starting in the early 1990s, we were no longer paid in won. Each of the families received a flat $120 a month. (In 2003, they switched us to 120 euros per month.) If we tried to buy all our food in dollar stores, however, the money wouldn't have lasted a week, so we needed a way to get some won. By that time, money was tight all over the country, so it was no problem to get our leaders to trade money for us on the black market, as long as they got a cut. This is an indication of how bad things had gotten by the 1990s. In decades past, a leader never would have participated in this type of corruption. It would have been our heads if they had found out, but now the leaders themselves were doing the exchanging. But their price was steep. It varied over the years, but often you could get twelve to fifteen hundred won per dollar on the black market, and the leaders would frequently take half of that.

Every month, I would change about $30 or $40 so I could buy staples like rice and flour from the government ration supply people who came once a month. Rice in North Korea is so dirty, you can wash it all you want and even after the fourth washing the water still looks like milk. It has bugs and stones in it. Sometimes the stones are so big and there are so many of them that I think they put them there on purpose to boost the weight. But at least it was usually edible. Those were the only foods that came reliably from the supply people. And toward the end, even those were less reliable. The flour stopped coming first, and then from the mid-1990s onward, sometimes the rice wouldn't come, either. But if the supply people brought eggs, it was guaranteed that half the eggs would be rotten. If they brought a frozen pig, measured by weight, you would discover later that they had stuffed the pig with water before freezing so more than half of your pig's weight was going to melt away into nothing.

All the rest of our food we had to get however we could, whether it was to buy, barter, or grow it. On my plot (which was about fifty by twenty-five feet), I could grow tomatoes, cucumbers, eggplant, red pepper, spinach, cabbage, garlic, and corn. We usually grew enough vegetables to make it through the year. We had an old Italian freezer, but it was a tricky juggling act to keep the vegetables from spoiling. If we got a full few days of electricity, the freezer would keep the food cool for four to five days. Then, if the electricity was out for a long time, you found yourself oddly wishing it was as cold as possible so you could move the frozen food outside to keep. So we would be cold as hell, but we would be glad that at least the food was not spoiling. There are always silver linings, I suppose.

Our biggest field was of corn. We would dry the corn on the roof of the house, and in a good year, I could grow 500 pounds of dried corn. That was a popular thing to trade. I could trade dried corn for moonshine or corn noodles. I grew so much corn so we could save all of our rice for Mika and Brinda. We had to send 60 kilograms (or 132 pounds) of rice to school every month. That's 2.2 pounds per daughter every day, even though a student's ration is only a pound per day, so you can see that someone, somewhere, was skimming more than half of what we sent. But that's just the way North Korea works. Growing all that corn allowed my wife and I to have corn noodles for lunch every day of our lives for more years than I care to remember. There is no food in the world that I am more sick of than corn noodles. I will never eat another corn noodle as long as I live.

In the 1990s we saw a noticeable difference in the desperation of people because of hunger. Stealing was always a problem in North Korea. If you didn't watch your things, someone would always be happy to relieve you of them. But with the food shortages of the 1990s, hunger drove both the people and the army to bolder and more desperate extremes. It became a routine for us as the corn ripened to pull all-night guard watches because otherwise the army would pick us clean. And on the nights before the first, the eleventh, and the twenty-first of every month, we also stood watch all night. Those were the eves of market days, and locals looking to sell anything they could get their hands on would clean us out of everything we were growing if we let them. Begging also became common. People would come to our house asking for food. If our food situation allowed us to help them, we would. If we couldn't, we couldn't. One time a soldier came to Siham's door begging for anything she could spare. That shocked us. It was one thing for the army to steal. But for a soldier to beg? That is something that never would have happened in decades past, when the country could at least feed itself.

In 1995 some cadres came by and told us, "Thanks to the great benevolence of Kim Jong-il, we are sending all of your children to the Foreign Language College in Pyongyang." That is when I knew that the Organization intended to turn all of our kids into spies. I don't believe that they had this plan from the very beginning. I don't believe that we were part of a spy "breeding" program or anything like that. But I do believe that once we all started to have families, someone got to thinking about it and realized what they had in us. It was certainly obvious to me once I started thinking about it. Consider: Few people in the outside world even knew that we Americans were in the country. Fewer still realized that we were married, and even fewer than that knew we had children. Just looking at them, it dawned on me pretty early on that our children would be the perfect raw material for North Korean spies, simply because they looked nothing like how a person would expect a North Korean spy to look. Dona and Dresnok's kids looked like Europeans. Siham and Parrish's kids looked like Middle Easterners. And Hitomi and my girls looked like Asian Americans.

Imagine how powerful, because it was so unexpected, a North Korean spy with Asian American features would be? There are so many children of South Koreans and American GIs running around South Korea. My girls could have poked around Seoul and U.S. Army installations throughout South Korea endlessly without arousing any suspicion, certainly less suspicion than young adults who look fully Korean. They could show up at a personnel office, for example, saying they were trying to track down their father who had skipped out on their South Korean mother. Isn't there anything the U.S. Army could do to help, any procedure for requesting records that might help them find their father? Now imagine how much more potent, because they are even more unexpected, the children of Dresnok and Dona, Parrish and Siham—all of whom do not have an ounce of Asian blood in them—would be doing spy work for North Korea in Europe, the Middle East, or even the United States.

For that reason, I was against them going to the Foreign Language College the second I heard the plan. (The school is sort of misnamed since it also has high school–level classes in addition to being a college.) Now, I should say that my girls had a long way to go—perhaps a decade or more of training—in political indoctrination, language skills, and spy craft—before they could even come close to being competent spies. They hadn't bought into the ideology enough, for starters. Even that would have taken years more. But it is widely known that enrollment at the Foreign Language College is a well-trod first step toward eventually becoming a spy. Take, for example, Kim Hyon Hui, the North Korean spy who posed as a Japanese tourist when she boarded Korean Airlines Flight 858 in Baghdad on November 29, 1987, and hid a bomb onboard that exploded in midair and killed all 115 people aboard. Her first step in a decade of spy training was to graduate from the Foreign Language College.

And the Organization was certainly not above dropping hints about what they had in mind. A cadre once told Dresnok that as soon as Gabi graduated from the Foreign Language College, Dresnok would probably never see his son again. And to me, one of our chiefs of staff would often say, "If we have learned one thing, it is that girls make the best revolutionaries." ("Revolution-ary" is a standard North Korean word for "spy.") "That's what we need," he would continue. "Female revolutionaries." He never mentioned my daughters, but he didn't have to. The hint was too obvious to miss.

So I argued against it the best I could. I wanted them to stay at the farm school. But there was no way to fight this one. When the Organization decided where my children were going to be educated, that was that. Nahi, Ricardo, Mika, Gabi, and Michael enrolled in the fall of 1995. But they only lasted three months. Since the school didn't have any dorm rooms for our kids at that time, they had to commute. Every morning, I would row them forty minutes down the river in a rowboat to the place where the bus would pick them up. But when it started getting colder and the river was too frozen to row but not frozen enough to walk, we all were screwed. The school and the Organization didn't have any solution for us, so we had to yank them out of school. For the next two years, Mika and the older kids didn't do any studying at all. Actually, they did very little of anything during this time (though I did have a little more help with the boiler, the water pump, and the farming). While they were out of school, Brinda and Ricky continued to study at the farm school, which explains why Brinda and Mika are now in the same academic class.

When Brinda and Ricky got to the senior high school age, the Organization must have decided that now that all seven kids were ready, their higher education should really begin. In the fall of 1997, the Organization provided us with a fifteen-passenger Nissan van, whose exclusive use was to ferry our kids back and forth from university.

Before that, however, we had two significant deaths in our families. In mid-1996, Dona was diagnosed with lung cancer. It was so far gone, they said, that there was little to do for her. She came home, and her health declined rapidly. She lingered on for six months, and during the last few she was in tremendous pain. My wife would go down and give her injections of morphine every night. She finally died in January of 1997. Fulfilling her wishes—she always said she did not want to be buried in Korea—Dresnok had her cremated.

In 1999, Dresnok remarried a half-Korean, half-Togolese woman named Dada. Dada was the daughter of a North Korean woman and a high-ranking politician's son from Togo, a small African country. Her father was, Dada said, a diplomat and the son of a former Togolese vice president. When the Togolese government was overthrown in January 1967, he fled North Korea, leaving his family, including Dada and her mother and sister, behind. Parrish met the sisters at the movie studio in 1995 where they were acting and told Dresnok about them. A couple of years after Dona had died, Dresnok said to the Organization, "Why don't you send me one of them?" It took a little while to arrange, but sure enough, she showed up after a while and moved into Dresnok's house. Within a few weeks they were as good as man and wife. They had a son named Tony, who is now six. As far as I know, they all still live at the farm or in Pyongyang.

Later in 1997, Parrish developed kidney trouble. He had a history of kidney stones dating back from when he was a young man before he crossed the DMZ, and his kidneys acted up throughout his life. He was in and out of hospitals all the time. He went into the hospital for treatment in early August. It was getting to be a routine, and he didn't think much about it. I came to see him on the day of his release. The doctor pulled me aside and said Parrish was much worse than he had ever been. He told me that he was basically a goner and that they were releasing him because there was nothing left they could do. They did not tell Parrish. In North Korean hospitals, they never tell the patient the truth about what is wrong, especially if the patient is going to die. Parrish came home, but true to the doctor's prediction, he started declining rapidly. Within a week or two, Parrish checked himself into the hospital again, sometime between August 17 and August 20. He died in the hospital on August 25. We buried him two yards away from Abshier.

The Foreign Language College was supposedly a high-class place where the country's elite were educated. One of Mika's best friends, for example, was the granddaughter of Kim Yong-nam, who has been both foreign minister and chief of the Korean People's Assembly, making him one of the longest-serving and highest-ranking officials in the country. But North Korea's version of high class is not the same as other countries'. The place was a hotbed for thieves. Tales of clothing and possessions getting stolen were common, and Gabi for one would pack up practically everything he owned every time he came home for the weekend.

Likewise, it is hard to think of the school as a land of plenty when the girls were always coming to me saying that school officials had requested a certain amount of supplies from every student's family. Sometimes they would say their teachers told them they needed to bring in 2 kilograms (4.4 pounds) of brass each by Monday. Or a kilogram of lead. Or a hundred meters of copper wire. They asked for coal, gasoline, even rabbit skins. And they told the students, "We don't care how you get it, just get it," which meant they were telling them to steal if they had to. So rather than turn my daughters into thieves, I became a pack rat. I saved everything that might have scrap value. I saved faucets, ball bearings, shattered glass scraps, rubber tubing, wood chips, you name it. You never knew what they were going to ask for.

By the late 1990s, then, our life had settled into this routine. I was resigned to this: My daughters were going to become spies who, within a few years, we might never see again. Hitomi and I would live out the rest of our days the way we had been for nearly two decades. We would live in Li Suk, we would farm, we would have each other, and we would make the best of what we had. And we would die in North Korea. I was 100 percent certain of that—until September 17, 2002, happened.

8 | Hitomi's Escape

At first, September 17, 2002, seemed like an ordinary night. Hitomi and I were at home alone together after a quiet day. Our daughters were at school, so we were just watching TV, as we did many evenings, before turning in for bed. When the news came on, the newscaster said that the day's big event was Japanese prime minister Junichiro Koizumi's visit to Pyongyang, which had just ended. His one-day summit with the Dear Leader had, of course, been a great success and brought great glory upon the North Korean nation (every newscast was never-ending propaganda). Among the many topics of discussion, the newscaster continued, the two men discussed the fates of Japanese citizens who were living in North Korea and how to return them to their homeland. The news person was vague, making it sound like they were talking about some of the Japanese who were stranded here after World War II or after the Korean War, but I got a feeling they were talking about the abductees. I said to Hitomi, "This has got something to do with you." But she said, "No way."

She did not think that Kim would ever discuss such a subject so publicly.

I ran into the closet, where I hid a portable radio that I used to listen to outside news broadcasts. I kept my radio secret from the Organization by storing it under some loose floorboards. Dona had gotten the radio years before from some Syrian exchange students, and I inherited it after she died in 1997. Usually, I tried to get the English-language broadcasts of NHK, Japan's public broadcaster, since it spent the most news time on relations between China, Japan, and the two Koreas. Unfortunately, NHK wasn't coming in very well that night, but I could pick up Voice of America. Its top story: Koizumi confronts Kim over abductees. I said, "God damn! I knew it!" I called Hitomi over and gave her one side of the earphones. Since her English is not very good, I translated the broadcast for her. The news report said that Kim had admitted for the first time that North Korea had, for decades, stolen Japanese citizens to use in its spy programs. What's more, Kim Jong-il had even admitted that five of these Japanese abductees were still alive and living in North Korea.

We were speechless. We couldn't believe it was all coming out so fast and so out of the blue. But those reports that first night were a little depressing for an unexpected reason: It was clear from the Voice of America's report that the Japanese government and media were surprised Hitomi even existed. The four other Japanese people that North Korea had said were alive were on the roster of suspected abductees that the Japanese government had submitted to North Korea in advance of the summit, the radio report said. But the fifth, this woman named Hitomi Soga, was not on the list. Who is she? Why was she not on the list? Why did the Japanese government not know anything about her? You could hear the reporters scramble for any information on this unknown woman, saying that they would follow up with details as they received them.

To this day, I believe that the very highest levels of the North Korean government were miscommunicating about Hitomi and me. Someone, somewhere, missed the fact that we were married to each other, or she never would have showed up on North Korea's list of living abductees submitted to Koizumi that day. I think our existence caused, and continues to cause, North Korea so much trouble that if government officials had realized that no one in Japan knew Hitomi was an abductee, and if they had stopped to think twice about the consequences for them that I was her husband, they would have just remained silent about her, and we both would still be rotting in North Korea now.

By the middle of the next day, most of the outside radio networks I could tune in to had pieced the story of Hitomi's life together. By the time I could get NHK in the evening, they knew not just the details of Hitomi's abduction in 1978 but also that she was married to me, the mysterious American defector. I was impressed. I had no idea where they had gotten all this new information, but they had most of the story correct. As we finished listening to the news that night, we didn't know what it all meant or what was going to happen to us, but we did know that some cadres would be coming for us soon. Frankly, we were worried.

The next day some cadres arrived to pick up Hitomi and me to go shopping in Pyongyang. Along the way the cadres said my wife had to make a detour for a meeting at the Foreigners' Hospital. There, she met with the North Korean Red Cross. They made it sound like the Organization was thinking about sending her to Japan for a visit as a reward for being such a good girl and model citizen. My wife had to just sit there and play along. "Oh, really?" she said. "That's nice. What a surprise!" and so on. The North Koreans made no mention of Koizumi's visit or the abductees issue. They just told her to make sure to tell me that she might be going away for a little while soon. "Oh, okay," she told them.

Less than a week later came the upheaval we had been waiting for. Some cadres showed up and told us that all four of us were going to stay at a guesthouse in Pyongyang for a few days. Mika and Brinda, who were at school at the time, met us at the guesthouse. They had always known that my wife was a Japanese abductee, but they didn't know that there had been this breakthrough. They knew something strange was going on, though, so as soon as we could get them alone, we told them what had happened. But we warned them not to let on, since we weren't supposed to know why we were there yet either.

One of the first things the cadres did upon our arrival in Pyongyang was to hand my wife a hundred-dollar bill. The next morning, we went downtown, and I'll be damned if my wife didn't spend almost all that money. Things were getting so crazy, her attitude was, "Who knows what will happen tomorrow?" At that time, we were receiving $120 every month, so $100 was a lot of money. She bought me a shirt and Brinda a pair of shoes. Later that afternoon, she had a meeting with a Japanese government delegation at the Koryo Hotel. That's where she got filled in on enough of the story that we didn't have to pretend that we didn't know what was going on anymore. The Japanese interviewed her and took DNA samples to verify her identity. They told her about the summit and what a large controversy the abductees issue had become and that the Japanese government was trying to find a way for the abductees and their families to come to Japan. It was there she also learned the basics of her family story since she had been away. They told her that her mother had never been heard from again (which surprised her), that her father was alive and still living on Sado (which almost surprised her more), and that her sister was married and living in Niigata.

The next day, the cadres marched us down to the Potong River Hotel to take some photos that the Japanese delegation, who were leaving that evening, could take with them. There was a sign that said "One-Hour Photo Processing," but it typically took all day to get the photos done. I told the leader, "This is going to make North Korea look like a bunch of asses. The whole country can't even get some photos made." The chief of staff had to go down and raise some hell to get the pictures finished before the Japanese plane left.

After three days, we went back home to Li Suk and waited. At that time, there was no doubt in Hitomi's mind and mine that she was coming back at the end of the visit. Despite all the unthinkable things that had happened in just the past week, the thought that she would stay in Japan, or that Mika, Brinda, and I would one day follow her, was not something that any of us realistically considered. It just wasn't possible that she could simply not return, so we did not talk about the future beyond the trip very much at all.

Around October 5, some cadres arrived in a tizzy and told us we were moving to Pyongyang—that day. We had to pack up everything we owned, down to the rice bowls and chopsticks, in a few hours. They moved us to an apartment in a regular, twelve-story apartment block in Pyongyang. They wanted any Japanese delegation that might visit to think that we lived just like regular

North Koreans. I don't know why or what purpose that would serve. The place was a dump. No Japanese delegation came to visit anyway. Around this time, we were told that the two governments had agreed to send Hitomi to Japan for what was supposed to be a ten-day to two-week visit.

Not long after we moved into that apartment, my family and I went to dinner with a high cadre at a guesthouse in Pyongyang. He gave my wife $1000 and two Kim Il-sung pins, one for me and one for her. He told her to spend at least $300 in Korea on gifts for people back in Japan. We went out shopping as instructed. My wife got a perm and a new suit for $25. That was the suit she wore when she got off of the plane. She bought a flower vase for $48 and three watches, one for her father, one for her sister, and one for her brother-in-law. "I am sure that everybody in your family has watches," I said. "And they sure don't need any more Seikos," which is what one of them was, "since they're Japanese anyway." She said, "I know, but there is nothing to buy in North Korea."

When our chief of staff got a look at what we had bought, he was appalled. "This stuff is trash," he said. "You can't take this stuff to Japan. Let me take care of it." So he came back a few days later, after getting permission to buy or take stuff from a Workers' Party warehouse, supposedly one of the same places they get the gifts that Kim Jong-il gives to foreign dignitaries. I believe it, because he came back with some of the most amazing and beautiful goods I had ever seen in North Korea. He brought back three white vases and three black vases, three embroidered silk wall hangings (one of Kung Gang Mountain, which is a famous peak along the North-South border), seven different bolts of fabric, forty bottles of wine, and a bunch of other stuff. In all, it came out to be about seven boxes full of antiques and precious objects. He was under orders to find us suitable gifts, but I'd be willing to bet he got in trouble later for overdoing it.

On the morning of October 15, my wife got up and left early with a cadre to do an obligatory ritual: pay tribute with two low bows and an offering of flowers to the sixty-five-foot bronze statue of Kim Il-sung in central Pyongyang. My daughters and I took an 8:00 A.M. bus to the airport. At the airport we went to a waiting lounge upstairs while my wife went into a meeting room on the first floor where the Japanese Red Cross was. Later, a Mercedes Benz pulled up with the four other Japanese abductees all together. I noticed that they had very little luggage, and suddenly I felt self-conscious that my wife had seven boxes of loot with her. They came inside and went to the same meeting room my wife was already in.

Upstairs, when one of the cadres from North Korea's Ministry of Foreign Affairs went fishing into his briefcase for some paperwork, I noticed he had a mess of cell phones in there. I asked him what they were for. He said they were for the Japanese. Each person would be issued a cell phone before leaving. Anytime they went anywhere, anytime they met someone, anytime they wanted to do something, they would have to call in to ask permission. "And what if they do nothing at all?" I asked. "They would still have to call in every twenty-four hours," he replied. I found out later that the phones were never distributed. The Japanese government just said no way.

After about thirty more minutes of waiting, a man from the Japanese foreign ministry came into the room and introduced himself. He said he was Akitaka Saiki, deputy director general of the Japanese Foreign Ministry's Asian and Oceanic Affairs

Bureau. He sat and chatted with me for another thirty minutes or so. He was very nice and spoke excellent English. He asked me about how my wife and I had met, the sort of work I did in North Korea, and the education Mika and Brinda were getting. I was very reserved in my answers. I assumed the room was bugged, and there were cadres everywhere anyway, so I didn't say anything that I didn't want the North Koreans to hear, and I assume he did the same. As he got up to leave, however, he asked me, "Do you think you would like to live in Japan?" I thought about the best way to phrase my response that gave a hint at my true feelings yet wouldn't get me in trouble. Finally, I said, "I think I would like Japan, but that would be impossible." He smiled and said, "We shall see."

Another Japanese, a woman, came in. Her name was Kyoko Nakayama, and she said she was a special adviser to the Japanese government and the head of the delegation. Looking at her the first time surprised the hell out of me. I had never seen an Asian with red hair before. No one in North Korea dyes their hair, and I didn't yet know that this was a very common practice in Japan. I greeted her in Korean, but from the look I got, I took it she didn't speak Korean, so I switched to English, which she could speak. We, too, talked about this and that. She told me not to worry and that she would take good care of my wife while she was gone.

As we finished talking, I noticed that she also said something about me going to Japan, which I took as another meaningful hint: "We would like you to come and visit." I couldn't think of anything safe to say, so I said, "I visited Japan before, a couple of times in 1960 and 1961 during my first tour of South Korea." She asked me where I had been, and I said, "Yokohama." Before she left, she said they had a souvenir for the girls. It was, she said, small, a trifle, a wooden Japanese doll, and she only had one, so the girls would have to share. I told her that was okay, and I thanked her.

The only other person around that day besides government people from the two countries, the abductees themselves, and my family was Kim Hae-gyun, the fifteen-year-old daughter of Megumi Yokota. I had never met her before and didn't talk to her much that day, except to exchange hellos.

Around noon, somebody announced that it was time to go, so the girls and I went downstairs to say a final goodbye to my wife. I said, "Kata-ora," which is a traditional Korean farewell, meaning, "Go and come back." I told her to say hello to everyone in her family for me and to take care of herself. The last thing my wife said to me was, "Wait for me." I said, "I don't have any women on the side. You know that. And I wouldn't get one even if I could." She said, "No, no. I mean, wait for me to have your next drink." She knew I was prone to overdrinking, but if she was around, she could always control me. She was partly making a joke and partly dead serious.

As she boarded the plane, the girls and I went out to the viewing deck on the tarmac to watch the plane take off. As I stood there and watched the chartered Japanese 767 fire up and taxi around the runway, despite all we had talked about and despite my confidence both before and after, I had a strong but momentary feeling that my wife would never return. My daughters and I stood there for a few minutes not saying a word, watching the plane leave, and then we turned around and headed inside.

On the way home, one of my leaders declared, "Let's have some wine!" I replied, "But my wife just told me to wait." He said,

"Never mind that. Let's get ten bottles! One for every day she is gone!" Well, we went to the store and I bought three bottles, not ten. We had lunch, and the driver asked, "What are you going to do if your wife doesn't come back?" I said, "Well, I guess I'll go to Japan." We just laughed and laughed, because at that time it was so impossible to contemplate that it was received as a joke.

During those first ten to fifteen days, the girls and I were just in a holding pattern, waiting for Hitomi to come back. And we really did think she was coming back. I would take the dog for long walks. The girls would go to school. Around this time, high-level diplomats from Japan and North Korea had a series of meetings in Malaysia, and the meetings were a bust. Japan offered to normalize relations if the North Koreans would answer all remaining questions about the abductees. The North Koreans said they had offered everything they knew, there was nothing more to say, and they thought the issue should be considered closed. That led to a stalemate.

My leader came to visit me one morning and told me to sit down. He said, "Twenty-two years of living together is a very long time, and to have it end like this." "What the hell are you talking about?" I asked. He said, "I don't know how to tell you this, but I don't think that your wife is ever coming back." "She said that?" I asked. "No," he responded, "but there was a meeting in Malaysia that did not go well. Japan is refusing to let any of the visitors return. Even though Hitomi wants to come back, Japan will not hand her over." "But they said she would be sent back no matter what," I yelled. "They guaranteed it!" "I know. I know," he said, "but they are not doing it now."

When I heard that news from my leader, it was like my world had ended. It hit me so suddenly: My wife and I, and our children, would be separated forever. Whether I had been naive up to now I don't know, but this development was actually quite unexpected, so it flattened me.

That is when I entered what was probably the darkest time of my life. I grew depressed, and I started drinking heavily. Throughout most of my time in North Korea, alcohol was scarce. If it was there, I would drink it, but on a day-to-day basis, there was usually less rather than more booze around. I, like many North Koreans, would supplement the sometimes scarce availability of the store-bought stuff with some moonshine others would make. I could trade two pounds of corn I had grown for a liter of moonshine. But here I often ran into the same economic issues: There was only so much corn, so there was only so much moonshine.

When my wife was gone, however, the cadres were interested in making sure I was "happy," so I could now get as much booze as I wanted. For the first few months of that separation, however, I still couldn't drink as much as I wanted. While I was living in the Pyongyang apartment building, Mika and Brinda were living with me and commuting to the Foreign Language College rather than staying in the dormitories. They limited my drinking almost as strictly as my wife did, so I could never really tear it loose when they were around. I had to at least function like a somewhat normal person in their presence.

In November, the cadres told me they wanted me to give an interview to a couple of Japanese journalists. A few days later, I met with two people from the Japanese magazine *Friday*. I was so mad that I ripped into the Japanese government fiercely. I blamed it for not living up to its end of the bargain. I said that the Japanese diplomat Saiki was a liar and did not follow through on the agreement he had made to send my wife back to North Korea.

Even so, my nerves were shot, and I was having frequent panic attacks, a condition I still suffer from but which was then at its peak. During the first week of December, I went back to Li Suk for a couple of days. I was having dinner at Siham's house when I started to hyperventilate. I felt a tightness in my chest, and my arms started to shake. Siham told me to go to the hospital, but I said, "No. I just need to go to bed." So I went to my house and tried to sleep, but I don't think I closed my eyes all night. In the morning, I told my leader, "I need to go to the hospital." I was admitted to the Foreigners' Hospital in the morning. They said I had had a nervous breakdown. I wound up staying in the hospital fifteen days. In the hospital, I had another press conference. The room was packed full this time, filled with Japanese TV crews. I hit the same theme again, practically shaking: "Why has Japan not lived up to its end of the deal!?" I asked. At one point, one of the journalists asked me if I wanted to go to Japan for treatment. I yelled, "You know damn well I cannot go to Japan!"

The day I was released, the chief of staff had a box with him that my wife had mailed me. Hitomi had given a parcel to the Japanese Foreign Ministry in Tokyo, who passed it on to the Japanese embassy in Beijing, who transferred it to the North Korean embassy in Beijing, who then sent it to Pyongyang. Inside the box was a coat and a sweater each for me, Mika, and Brinda and two letters. The first letter was written in late October. In it, Hitomi said she was frustrated by the lack of progress in finding a way that we could all be reunited, frustrated that her visit to Japan had stretched from ten to fifteen days to now being open-ended, and frustrated that sometimes it seemed like we might be separated permanently. The second letter was written twenty days later, and it mostly concerned my mother. Hitomi said she hadn't had any personal contact with my mother, but she had seen her on the news and it looked like she was well and that she hoped that I would be able to see her someday. She wrote that if she could do something to make that happen, she would. I broke down when I read those letters.

I quickly wrote a letter back to her in which I told her I missed her, and I brought her up-to-date on some of the things that had been going on, including my spell in the hospital. I gave the letter to the leader to send through the Foreign Ministry. The next day, my leader came back and said the foreign minister wouldn't send the letter because it included the sentence "Give my regards to Saiki." That sentence, the minister said, indicated too much identification and affection for the Japanese enemies. So I rewrote the whole letter without the offending line and gave it back in a huff.

I said, "Fuck this." I went home and dug out our old marriage license, which happened to have our home addresses on it. I wrote her another letter a little while later addressed directly to her on Sado Island, and I went down to the international post office in Pyongyang, one of only two post offices in all of North Korea that handle international mail, and posted it direct. I made sure to include the address of the apartment building in Pyongyang where I was living temporarily so she could try to mail me back directly as well. Well, I am still sort of amazed by this, but that letter got through to her no problem. After that first time, however, the Organization was on to that trick, and agents intercepted every letter I tried to send straight through the international post office.

I received the next letter from Hitomi in March, addressed directly to me at the apartment building in Pyongyang. She said she got the one from me through government channels on December 31 and the one I sent direct on February 13. She asked after my health and my heart. She mentioned that she was writing from the hospital herself where she had just undergone an operation to remove a spot of lung cancer doctors found. She said that it was small and that the doctors were confident they had licked it early, but she wanted to tell and reassure me herself so that I wouldn't be worried if I heard it from another place. She asked after the leaders, and she said she longed to see her family again. She mentioned that she was working with the Japanese government on appealing to the U.S. government to get me a pardon and to see if there wasn't some way that I could live in Japan. "I am very sorry that I cannot be there with you," she wrote. Between diplomatic channels, directly mailing each other on the sly, registered mail we received permission to send, and slipping letters to trusted people to hand-deliver, my wife and I estimate we each sent the other approximately thirty letters in the eighteen months we were separated. In all, we each received about seven or eight of those letters.

Later in March 2003, they moved me back to Li Suk. Why? I looked at it like this: If my wife wasn't coming back, then they didn't need to give a damn about me anymore, which was all fine by me. With my daughters back in the dorms at college and me living alone, there was nothing to stop me from being drunk almost all the time.

After moving back to Li Suk, I fell into a pattern of constant drunkenness. On Monday, I would go into town. The cheapest, nastiest booze I could find was Chinese ginseng liquor, which was eighty proof and came in five-liter jugs that cost $2.50. I would buy two jugs. I bought it at the Daesong Department Store in East Pyongyang, not far from the Romanian, Libyan, and Egyptian embassies. By Monday afternoon, I was home drinking by myself, and sometimes I would not wake up until Friday. Often, I would not recall a thing that had transpired from the week. Sometimes the dog would wake me up to get fed by licking my face, but that was about it. Many weeks, no one would come to my house for days, which was how I liked it. Every once in a while, Dresnok and Siham would drop by to see how I was doing. They even developed a joke about it. "Is he all right?" one would ask. "I don't know. He was passed out, face down on the floor," the other would say. "Well, at least he's alive, because two days ago he was passed out on the bed!" On Fridays, I had to straighten myself and the house up because the girls would come home for the weekend. I would spend the weekend relatively sober, and then, after they shipped back off to school, I would start the process all over again. In no time, whenever I walked into the department store, the liquor counter salesgirl had my order lined up as soon as she saw me. I did this routine, staying drunk, for a year straight.

By the spring of 2003, Hitomi and the other abductees had decided that they were not going to go back to North Korea, and on April 15, 2003, they had a press conference to declare as much. They said they had decided that there was no benefit to anyone if they returned, and they believed that the Japanese government would be successful in negotiating the handover of the rest of their families still stuck in North Korea, even me. Hitomi told me later that she had been convinced that with good diplomacy, patience, and pressure applied at the right places at the right time, chances were good for me to someday live as a free man.

The update I got from the leader about the press conference was a lie. He said that my wife and the others had had a press conference where they condemned the Japanese government for not being allowed to return to North Korea. I believed what he said absolutely. I was so furious that night that I sat down and wrote Koizumi a letter where I called him a son of a bitch and every other name in the book. I wrote, "To be kidnapped twice in one lifetime, that is just too much!" I marched down to the post office and mailed it myself. I assume it was never sent because I never heard about it again. I continued to think that Hitomi was not being allowed to return all the way up until I talked to her in person in Indonesia. I don't know how, in all of the secret news radio broadcasts that I listened to over the next fifteen months, I managed to miss that piece of information, but I did. My understanding of the April press conference just added more misery to my already miserable existence. It only intensified my desire to stay wasted all the time. Some mornings, I would wake up and my hands would be shaking so badly, I couldn't raise a coffee cup to my lips without spilling.

During my lost, drunken year, I definitely had a death wish. On New Year's Day, as is customary, I had to host some cadres. They came over, and I got drunk. After the party was over, I was talking to a few of them in my living room. I pointed to a picture of Kim Jong-il and said, "If it weren't for that son of a bitch, my family would be together now." I called Kim a *ga-sicki,* a dog, the worst curse imaginable. Being disrespectful to the official photos of Kim Jong-il and Kim Il-sung is one of the most serious crimes there is, and to curse one out is unthinkable. The punishment should be instant execution. Mika was there, and she just about died when she heard what I said. She tugged on my arm, pleading, "Papa, they are going to shoot you if you don't shut up." I don't know why they didn't, but they didn't. All I can come up with is that the leaders who were there that night were the few that I had grown to be closest to over many years, and they simply chose to look the other way.

The only thing that got me off the sauce was my prostate trouble. In the spring of 2004, I started having to get up and go to the bathroom every few minutes in the middle of the night. I went to the hospital, and they operated on me around April 15. Every night the leaders would come into my hospital room, sit on the floor, and play cards and drink while I was there with tubes sticking out of my belly and catheters running up my penis. In May, just as I was about to be discharged, one of the nurses came to tell me that Koizumi was coming back to North Korea. I told her that I was going to meet with that bastard while he was in town. I said, "I'm going to give him a good old-fashioned Korean cussing. That son of a bitch stole my wife." I went home and waited for Koizumi's arrival, which was less than a week away.

9 | My Escape

On the morning of May 22, Mika, Brinda, and I were picked up by a high cadre from the Ministry of Foreign Affairs and taken to an old country house of Kim Jong-il's about twelve miles outside of Pyongyang. That's where we were to meet with Prime Minister Koizumi.

We arrived about 9:00 A.M., three hours early, and were taken into a big waiting room where there was fruit on a silver platter and lots of soft drinks on a side table. In that room, over the next few hours, four high-ranking North Koreans I had never seen before came to talk to me. Each one gave me a long lecture, talking to me about what he said would happen to me and my daughters if I left that day. The last person to meet me was very high up, a vice minister of foreign affairs. All of them were singing the same song. They told me that the United States had no respect for me or my family and that I would spend the rest of my life in prison, if I weren't executed. They brought in faxes and photocopies of news reports from all over the world that suggested the United

States would have no mercy on me. (I don't know how many of those news reports were forged, since they had already been "translated" into Korean. I imagine some were but not all. One of the things that I have learned about reporters is that they are very good at stating things authoritatively, even when it is absolutely impossible for them to have any idea of what they are talking about.) The North Koreans also told me that my daughters would live intolerable lives, that they would be harassed and discriminated against wherever they went, and that they might even be in physical danger.

The North Korean officials never actually told me that they were forbidding me from leaving, but they didn't have to. They told me that if I decided to go to the airport, I would have to ride in a separate car with my family rather than on the buses that had carried the North Korean and Japanese delegations here. I got the unspoken message very clearly: I was not to leave that day, and if I tried, they would prevent it. People may doubt me on this point. People may say that the only reason I didn't leave that day was because I was afraid of getting arrested by the Americans once I landed in Japan. They can believe that if they want, but I know the truth. I have lived long enough in North Korea to pick up on signals, to hear the threats that are not actually spoken. I know in my heart if I had tried to get on that plane on that day, the North Koreans would have told the Japanese that I had changed my mind at the last minute, our car would have broken off from the convoy, and we would have been taken God knows where.

Just before noon, someone announced that Koizumi had arrived. We all got up and walked into a conference room. Koizumi came in with an entourage of about seven or eight people. No North Koreans came into the room. They waited just outside with the larger contingent of Japanese. Koizumi walked in, and I shook his hand. I told him it was a great honor to meet him. He sat down across from me and my daughters. There was a note-taker in the corner, two translators at Koizumi's side, and a couple of other Japanese diplomats hanging out around the edges of the room.

Then we launched in on what turned out to be a pretty testy debate. Remember that my family and I were still operating under the assumption that Hitomi was being held in Japan against her will. We had none of the information that the rest of the world considered common knowledge. I had no under-standing about how hard my wife was working on my behalf and how strongly all of Japan had rallied to her cause of reuniting her family. Even though I had been listening to foreign-language radio broadcasts as often as I could, very little of this part of the story was coming through. Every day now, I thank God for my wife, the Japanese people, and the Japanese govern-ment, and I know I am a free man because of them. Today, I have nothing but the highest respect, admiration, and gratitude for everything Koizumi has done for me and my family, persevering on our behalf even when it was politically risky for him to do so. But at that time, I was madder than hell at him.

As he sat down, Koizumi reached into his briefcase and handed me a letter written by my wife. I took it but did not open it right away. "You know why I am here, don't you?" he asked. "Yeah," I said. "You are here because you have my wife." Mika is a feisty one, and she jumped in almost immediately, asking, "Why haven't you let her come back like you promised?" Koizumi said, "I could never send her back to a country that had stolen her in the first place." "But this is where her home and her family are," she said. Koizumi responded, "I am here because I am trying to reunite her with her family." While Mika and Koizumi were fighting, I was able to read my wife's letter. In it, she told me to think very hard before making my decision, but she thought I should come with Koizumi.

I thought about the letter as I refolded it, and at the time I wondered if much of it had been coerced or if she was just saying what she knew Japan wanted to hear. I put the letter in my jacket pocket and joined the fight. I told Koizumi that my wife was kidnapped right now, in Japan. Koizumi said that that was not true. "She does not want to come back to North Korea," he said. "She wants you to come to Japan." I told him that if I came back with him, then I was going to go to jail for a very long time, a prospect I was not too happy about. Koizumi told me that he could not promise anything, but that he would do everything in his power to ensure I would receive fair and compassionate treatment from the United States.

At that point, one of his men passed him a note, which he read. He then ripped a piece of paper from a small notebook of his own. Looking at the note he had been passed, he wrote a new one in his own hand. He then passed me the note he had written across the table. It said, in English, "The Prime Minister of Japan will assure you that he will do the utmost that you can live together happily with Mrs. Jenkins in Japan." I read it, folded it, put it in my jacket pocket, and did not say a word.

Contrary to a number of news reports that followed this meeting, Prime Minister Koizumi did not make any guarantees regarding how I would be treated by the United States. He said only that he would do the best he could to request humane treatment for me, and that since the United States and Japan were best friends, he was confident that the United States would at least listen to his point of view. Also contrary to some news reports, I never asked Koizumi or anyone else from the Japanese government, during this meeting or at any other time, for a guarantee of a U.S. pardon before I would consider traveling to Japan. It is true that I was cautious and apprehensive about how the United States might treat me, and I asked the Japanese officials to do everything they could to help me, but I knew from the beginning that if I ever left North Korea, I would have to face the U.S. Army myself, and I never insisted that Japan work a deal for me.

Following this, Koizumi said, "Kim Jong-il has said you can go." Mika piped up again: "Is that really true?" Koizumi pulled out a piece of paper signed by Kim Jong-il saying so, and he placed it right between me and Mika. Throughout the whole meeting, Brinda didn't say a word. I was glad, because the thing she was most likely to say was "Let's go to Japan!" and that would have caused all kinds of trouble. The North Koreans originally told us we would have about ten minutes with Koizumi, but the whole conversation wound up taking an hour. At the end of it, I told him that I appreciated all of his efforts, and he certainly gave me a lot of new stuff to think about, but there was simply no way that we were going to be able to come with him to Japan that day.

Realizing we had hit the end, he signaled for one of his people to come over and introduce a new topic. "There is one more thing we could try," said this Japanese diplomat. "Would you be willing to meet your wife in a third country, maybe China, in a little while, where you could all discuss further what, as a family, you would like to do?" I said, "Yes. That sounds like a very good idea. Let's do that." As we were parting, the Japanese gave us a few gifts: a disk of cartoon videos for the girls, an inspirational book in English about a Japanese who overcomes adversity despite being born without any arms and legs, and a carton of Mild Seven cigarettes for me.

As we were walking out, I told Koizumi that I wished we could have spoken in English without interpreters, since I knew that he had studied in England. He looked surprised that I knew that and smiled. I also told him that I loved Japan when I visited Yokohama in 1960 and 1961. He threw up his hands in celebration, as if to say, "That's great!" I was hoping he would let loose with some English, but he never did. Through his interpreter, he said that he was sorry it didn't work out this time and that he held out hope that I would be able to come to Japan someday. I said, "We shall see."

After that meeting, they moved me to a guesthouse rather than back to my house in Li Suk as everybody tried to arrange the next meeting. Word got back that my wife wouldn't do the meeting in China (which, in retrospect, was probably a wise choice). Someone suggested Singapore. I said no, since I thought it was too close an ally of the United States. Finally, someone said, "How about Indonesia?" Indonesia sounded like a fine choice to me, a very neutral country.

In preparation for the meeting in Indonesia, I had to decide what I was going to do in the face of all of the variables converging around me. Through it all, the one priority that I never deviated from is that I would try to keep my family together no matter what. If my wife wanted to return to North Korea, then that was that: North Korea was where we would stay. If, however, she wanted to return to Japan, then I would do everything

I could to make sure Mika, Brinda, and I could get to Japan. If part of that arrangement required me to throw myself at the mercy of the U.S. government, to whom I was a wanted man, then so be it. If all the other factors required that I went to jail for life, then I went to jail for life. I decided that very early on.

For most of this time, however, I was convinced that Hitomi wanted to come back to North Korea. I was operating under the mistaken assumption that Hitomi was being held against her will in Japan. But still, I had to prepare mentally for the possibility that Hitomi was not coming back and that we would follow all the other families to Japan. There was no way I was going to allow my daughters to be permanently split from their mother. I knew that going to Japan was the best prospect for the family, though it was the riskiest for me. I desperately wanted to get my children out of North Korea. And if there was an opportunity to get my daughters off of the spy route I was sure they were traveling down, I was going to take it. But for me to return to North Korea without them was out of the question. And without my wife and my daughters in North Korea, I was as good as dead anyway. So I resolved, if it came to that, to turn myself in, to go along with the wishes of my wife and to ensure that my daughters had a chance at a free, happy, and prosperous life.

The North Koreans, meanwhile, were doing everything in their power to ensure that I would come back with both my wife and kids. In order to do that, they promised me that we would all live like royalty. They promised me a new car with all the gasoline I wanted, a fully furnished new house in the middle of Pyongyang, new clothes, and a new television. They told me they would bury me in the patriot's cemetery and drove me there to see the plot. (They also showed me the graves of four

Japanese buried there. I saw them. I don't know who they were, but I think they might have been part of the Red Army faction.) They told me everything I wanted would be Kim Jong-il's gift. They got me a new suit of clothes for the trip. June 1 is Mika's birthday, and they threw her one hell of a lavish twenty-first birthday party. There were only a handful of people there, but they provided a huge spread of fish, meats, fresh vegetables, and drinks. They gave her a watch and teddy bear. As part of their campaign to get me to return with the whole family, they even gave me an eighteen-karat gold wedding band to give to my wife in Indonesia.

The only thing to do with the cadres was to play along. I had to pretend that I would do everything in my power to convince my wife to return to North Korea when we were in Indonesia. But I also had to pretend that even if I couldn't convince Hitomi to come back, there was no doubt that I was coming back with my daughters. At the same time, I had to thwart their attempts to take out "insurance" that we would come back by, for example, letting only one of the girls go to Indonesia. I told them no way, that both girls were going. If they had split up the family like that, there was a good chance it would have been split permanently.

On June 21, I got another letter from my wife, this one hand carried by a representative of a Japanese NGO. In the letter, my wife told me that she had waited for us to come on May 22. She thought I would come and was disappointed that I didn't, but she could understand why. She said she was looking forward to meeting in Indonesia and that once we were there, we could decide at our own pace where we should live. First of all, she said, the four of us needed to reunite. And then we could discuss our future at our own pace. "We four can live with no problems regardless of where we wind up," she wrote. "I am sorry that I missed being with the family on Mika's birthday, but we will not fail to be together on Brinda's on July 23. May the days go very fast until we meet again."

If the North Koreans tried harder than ever to charm me into staying during the two months between the meeting with Koizumi and leaving for Indonesia, they also tried harder than ever to scare the hell out of me about the United States. They continued to show me all these news stories from the West about what the United States planned to do to me and how there would be no mercy for me. Even Dresnok got in on the act. Those final few months, he would come over for coffee as often as he could. He said he didn't have his radio anymore, so he always wanted to talk about the news. He was just speaking his mind. I don't think the cadres coached him on what to say, but he would always tell me how the army was going to string me up and send me to jail for life. Considering my nerves at the time, his opinion didn't help much, but I understood where he was coming from. I think in both of our minds we were seriously considering that I might never be coming back, though we could never discuss that, and a big part of him was afraid of being lonely. We would sit at a table, drinking coffee, mostly silent since we didn't know who was listening and couldn't say all the things we wanted to say. He would often say something about us being the only two left, but he would never finish the sentence.

During this time, Brinda was already bugging me to leave and not come back. Whenever we were alone, she would tug on my arm and say, "Let's go. Let's get out of here. Let's go to Japan." I would always tell her to be quiet, that she couldn't say such things out loud. Mika was different. She believed more of the propaganda back then. I don't know why, but she was a bit more indoctrinated at that point, so I had to be careful about what I said around her regarding any doubts I had as to whether we were coming back.

I tried to prepare for both possibilities. I had to make it look like I was coming back yet also be ready if we didn't. The trick was to bring things that were important but didn't look important. The problem was that I couldn't get back to the house in Li Suk long enough and often enough to be able to pick stuff carefully. I wanted to bring Megumi's bag, for example, but I couldn't get to it. In the end, all I was really able to bring was my wedding license and a few dozen photographs.

Some of the photos did turn out to be valuable later. One roll was from May or June. We had to shoot photos of everybody in the apartment building for new citizenship papers: Dresnok, Siham, my daughters, Nahi, Michael, Ricky, and Gabi. Everybody was there but Ricardo. After shooting head shots of everyone, we had some of the thirty-six exposures on Dresnok's camera left over, so I took some snaps. Once I got to Japan, these were the only photos I had of what the "Western" North Koreans in my little community looked like. I believe that these photos and other information I provided helped me earn a more lenient sentence from the army by convincing prosecutors and investigators that I was sincere in my remorse for deserting and by helping to prove that I would do whatever I could to help America now.

The night before we left, I had dinner with a high cadre at the guesthouse in Pyongyang. Before I left, he gave me five bottles of ginseng liquor to give away as gifts, a carton of Marlboro cigarettes, and $2,000 cash. The next morning, July 8, they picked me and my daughters up, and we paid our respects to the giant statue of Kim Il-sung. We then went to the airport and waited. It wasn't long before a chartered All Nippon Airways plane pulled up. We got on the Boeing 767. It was a half or a quarter filled. On board, there were Japanese and Korean government people. They had set up a smoking section about midway back on the plane. Mr. Saiki said it was a special concession for the chain-smoking Koreans.

About halfway through the flight, I was smoking, and one of the leaders joined me. "It will be good to see your wife," he said. "Yes, it will," I said. "You have a lot of family in Japan," he said. "I suppose I do," I said. "It is good to have family," he said. "Yes, I suppose it is," I said. I didn't know exactly where he was heading with this, but I had a feeling. The ashtray was a plastic cup half-filled with water. As he leaned over to drop the butt into the cup, he said to me very quietly, "If you don't come back, there is nothing we can do."

Once we touched down in Jakarta, my wife was there on the tarmac along with throngs of media. She arrived a day or two before we did. She met me on the stairs of the plane, and as I stumbled down the steps, I fell into her arms, and she planted a big kiss on me. I was a little surprised, but not as much as I have been told the Japanese were, who it seems found this extreme display of affection a little shocking. As a joke these days, she denies she did this, saying that I grabbed her, but my daughters always interject, "Mama, that's a lie! They have pictures! The whole world saw it! You grabbed him!"

The bus ride into the city took two hours. I had never seen such a bad traffic jam in my life. In Pyongyang there was rarely any traffic at all, even in the center of the city, but here the streets were jammed with cars. I did not wait long before getting down to business with my wife. I had already been waiting so long, I didn't see any reason to delay the discussion any further. The bus was full of the Japanese delegation, so I still had to be a little discreet. We sat side by side, not looking at each other while we talked. "Why didn't you want to have this meeting in China?" I asked. "If we met in China," she said, "I may have been sent back to North Korea." So I asked, "You don't want to go back to North Korea?" "No," she said quietly but firmly. "But I thought you did," I said. "The Organization told me that you have been trying and wanting to come back this whole time." "Gae-so-ri," she said. (That is dog talk.) "Well," I thought, "that's it, then. The decision has been made. We are not going back."

They put us up in a hotel downtown that was the nicest place I think I have ever stayed. We were in a suite on the fourteenth floor. It was larger than any house I had ever lived in. Brinda and Mika were in a state of shock. The television just blew them away. Actually, it blew me away, too. All those channels. The size of it. The brightness of all the colors. Some of the stuff that was shown, and the fact that it was on twenty-four hours a day. I think that was their very first whiff that there might be a lot more to the outside world than the North Koreans had ever told them. It didn't take them long to sense that the rest of the world was much more free than North Korea had been. At the same time, there was only so much freedom for us: There was a guard on our door (officers from the Niigata police force, to be specific) twenty-four hours a day. Right across the hall from us was the Japanese delegation, including Saiki and Nakayama.

The next morning, my wife and I continued the discussion we had been having on the bus. To test her resolve on the matter, I said to her, "If you are not going back, then there is no point to me being here. The girls and I will go to China for a little while and then return to North Korea to pick up our new house. I don't see what the problem is for you to come to North Korea. The Organization says you can go and come as you please. You can take the ferry back and forth. You can visit anytime you want." She responded, "You know one big reason why I am not going back? It is not just because of me. It is because of you. Because of your family in the United States. If you go back to North Korea, you will never see your mother and sisters again." "But I am not going to see them anyway, since I am going to go to jail for life!" I yelled. "You are not going to go to jail!" she yelled back. "How can you say that?" I asked. "You can't say that for sure." I had realized by then that she and Koizumi were doing everything they could to appeal to the Americans for understanding and leniency in my case, but I also knew that my wife was in no position to offer me assurances about how the U.S. Army was going to choose to punish me. Whenever it was I had to face my accusers, I knew at least on that count, I would be doing it alone.

It was around that time I also realized that the power between my wife and me had changed. In North Korea, I was primarily responsible for protecting her and providing for her, and she would do what I thought was best for us almost without exception. She needed me. Now, however, the equation had changed. I would have to listen to her; she would be my guide. I now needed her more than she needed me. This change in our relationship has been one of the most noteworthy parts of our lives together since 2002, and, to be honest, sometimes one of the hardest for me to adjust to.

Not long after that conversation with my wife, we called the Japanese delegation in to tell them our news: We had decided not to return to North Korea. We had a meeting and discussed where we were going to live, my fears of the U.S. government taking me by force, things like that. We had little meetings like that often over the eight or nine days we were in Indonesia.

It would be wrong to assume from the way that I am talking about this that any of these decisions were easy or that I was not feeling a tremendous amount of anxiety. On that second night, my nerves were a mess. I drank two bottles of the ginseng liquor that the high cadre had given me the night before I left. As liquor tends to do, it made me feel good at first. I asked my wife if she wanted to go dancing downstairs at the cabaret they had at the hotel. She said, "Hell, no." I said, "Suit yourself. I'm going down."

I started to walk out the door, but the guard at the door wasn't letting me out. I told him to get out of the way. Before I knew it, there were four Japanese at the door, and the argument moved into the suite. I said, "You are not the bosses of me. I am not Japanese. You cannot tell me what to do." They didn't speak much English or Korean, but they were not budging. I started yelling, "I spent forty years being a prisoner and now I am a prisoner again? Who do you think you are? Get the hell out of my way!" They kept talking, and talking turned to yelling, and then the pushing started. A government official, someone I had never seen before (and never saw again), moved to the front. I grabbed his necktie with two hands—at the end and at the knot— putting him in a hold. He wasn't going anywhere. They pulled me off of him, which was a good thing, since I can't imagine what I would have done to him next. I realized it could not escalate any further without there being big problems. Saiki had showed up by that time and yelled, "If you don't sit down and stay where you are for the rest of the night, I will turn you over to the Americans right away!" I told Saiki, "Go ahead. I know the Americans can't touch me here!" But after I had calmed down, I told them, "It's fine. I'm not going to the bar."

I understand now that the Japanese were only doing what they needed to do, and that the biggest concern was not my freedom or even my safety but unfavorable attention from the press. I was being scrutinized much more closely by the Japanese press than I realized, and the government and the guards were really just looking out for my best interests. After forty years in North Korea, I didn't even know how the press worked, and to this day, dealing with the press is not something I am good at or comfortable with. It is one of the most challenging and wearying parts of living in Japan today. I know that rumors of the scuffle have leaked out since then, and none of it reflects very well on me, but believe it or not, the Japanese delegation didn't mention it the next morning, and, in fact, they never brought it up again.

A few days into our stay, we met the Japanese ambassador to Indonesia and had dinner at his house. During that dinner, someone from the house staff told me that I had a phone call and showed me to the living room. I honestly had no idea who it was, though I suspected it was someone from the North Korean delegation wanting to check up on me. I got on the line, and it was my sister Pat, calling from Weldon, North Carolina. "What's up, Bubba?" she asked. Bubba was her private name for me. Hearing that, I started to sob. I couldn't believe it. Even though all of these events were happening to me in such quick succession, that was the first time it really hit me that I was like a dead man who had come back to life. We were only able to talk for fifteen or twenty minutes, but we packed as much catching up into that time as possible. It was then that I learned that two of my sisters,

Olivia and Audrey, had died of cancer in the 1990s. The four others were doing well, though, as was my brother, Gene. Pat told me that our mother had heard that I had gotten out of North Korea and was asking, "Where's Robert? When is Robert coming home?" I told Pat to tell Mama that she needed to hold on but that I was going to get there just as soon as I could. I didn't know when, I said. I still had so many more obstacles to clear, but soon. After crying my way through that conversation, I told my sister I loved her and would talk to her soon.

Over the course of the rest of the week, I had been to the hospital once in Jakarta and got daily checkups from the two Japanese doctors seeing to me in the hotel to monitor how my recovery from the prostate surgery I had in April in North Korea was progressing. Other than that, there was a lot of waiting around while both sides finished their diplomacy. Near the end of the week, we had another meeting with the Japanese to finalize how we were actually going to get to Japan. The Japanese asked me if I wanted to stay in Indonesia any longer. I responded that as long as we had decided on the plan, we might as well get it over with. The Japanese said that either way, I needed urgent medical care as soon as possible, and if we went to Japan, I would need to go straight to a hospital in Tokyo as soon as we landed. I needed daily medical attention to clean my wound. It was not healing properly, and both Japanese doctors had become increasingly concerned about my condition. They said I needed a detailed medical examination and dedicated inpatient care.

Once we had decided on the plan for leaving Indonesia, I told Saiki that I needed to write the North Koreans a letter, telling them of my intentions. After I had slept on it, though, I decided that I needed to tell them in person. If there was one thing I have learned as a consequence of my desertion forty years ago, it's that the big decisions need to be confronted head-on. I had to face the North Koreans and tell them myself that my family was not coming back. Saiki said the next morning that he was relieved to hear me say so. He had been thinking that a face-to-face meeting was essential but for a different reason: Unless I told them in person, he said, the North Koreans could claim that a letter from me had been coerced or forged.

A few nights later, a man from the Indonesian Ministry of Foreign Affairs came and got Hitomi and me and brought us up to a meeting room on the thirty-fourth floor. My wife and I decided not to bring our daughters, mostly for fear that Mika might not just make a scene but declare that, as a twenty-one-year-old adult, she did not agree, could not be forced, and wanted to go back to North Korea. The North Koreans probably would have taken her up on it, and that would have been the end of that. The family would have been permanently split. We couldn't have that happen, so we didn't even tell the girls that we were going to this meeting. We just told them we had to go out for a little while, and we left them playing cards with some of the guards.

The Indonesians went down and got the three-person North Korean delegation. The Japanese government had set up a video camera in the corner. A man from the Indonesian Ministry of Foreign Affairs, an interpreter, one of the Japanese doctors, and the three Koreans were the only ones in the room besides me and my wife. We made small talk for a few minutes, and then I got down to business. I told them that none of us were going back to North Korea. I was expecting the worst, waiting for the outburst and the shouting and table pounding. But none of that happened.

They listened quietly, took it pretty well, and put up no fight. Within a few moments, they said that they had even expected this.

We wound up talking for about an hour, and it was one of the most pleasant conversations I can remember ever having with a bunch of North Koreans. They gave me a blue notebook. I gave them the two bottles of ginseng liquor that were left and the carton of Marlboros the high cadre had given me. I also handed them a model of a Boeing 747 that my wife had received as a gift on the plane. I said that Dresnok had wanted a souvenir and asked them to please give it to him. I hope they did. The North Korean delegation went back to North Korea that night. They did not even wait for us to leave for Japan.

Later that night, when we told Mika, she panicked. I had told Brinda a couple of days before, but I told her not to say anything to Mika, since I knew that Mika would take the news harder. I wanted to break it to Mika more slowly. I said to her, "I told you when we got on the plane that we were as good as on Japanese soil. And that is still true. Your mother has thought very hard about it, and she is not going back to North Korea. And I am not splitting up the family. So if she is not going back, then neither are we." Mika's biggest worry was what people back in Pyongyang would say. "Back in North Korea," she said, "they are all going to call me a traitor." I told her that everybody in America calls me a traitor, but almost no one knows the whole story. "If people knew everything," I told her, "they would probably think differently." She was not entirely soothed by this. In the end, I told her that she had no choice and would see eventually that we were making the right decision. I told her she simply had to trust us.

On July 18, we boarded a Japan Airlines charter bound for Tokyo. We got off the plane, packed into a bus, and went to the Tokyo Women's Medical University Hospital. I have been told that some people were surprised to see those photos and videos of me leaning on a cane as I walked from the plane to the bus. And since no one had ever seen me use a cane before, they assume it was all a big act. Here is the deeper story behind the cane: I was given a walking stick after my first visit to the Jakarta hospital and was encouraged to use it whenever I walked. Even though I was sick and in pain, I did not understand why I needed it, since despite all my medical problems, I did not really have trouble walking. But the doctors told me they had become very concerned that some of my internal incisions, which were not healing properly, would tear open if I was not extremely careful, and the cane would alleviate pressure on my internal organs. So until I made it to the hospital, I used the cane to support my walking. At the hospital, they put me in a large room in a private wing that was heavily guarded. They also provided an adjoining room for my wife and daughters to live in while I was being treated.

Even though no one was certain how long I would need to be hospitalized, I was soon looking ahead to my legal problems. I knew that after I was well, and that would be sooner rather than later, I was going to have to face the fact that I was a wanted man. Every time that we cleared one hurdle, there was always another one up ahead. Now that I was safely in the hospital room, I still wasn't particularly safe. I had no idea what would happen next. Since I had no money, I knew I could not afford a lawyer. I did not even know what crimes I was actually accused of. My plan, since I didn't know what else to do, was to plead guilty to absolutely everything the U.S. Army accused me of, no matter what it was, even stuff I didn't do, and just throw myself upon their mercy.

About a week or so after arriving at the hospital, I received a letter from something called Trial Defense Services (TDS). I had no idea such a thing existed. The way the letter described it, TDS was a branch of the U.S. Army's legal department that acted like the public defender's office does for civilians accused of crimes in the United States who cannot afford their own lawyers. I knew about public defenders, but I didn't think that there were independent lawyers in the U.S. Army who defend soldiers at no cost to the soldier. I thought odds would be stacked against an accused soldier like me. I didn't think the army would consider me having a qualified lawyer a priority. So getting a free lawyer provided by the government seemed too good to be true.

A few days after receiving the letter from TDS, I got a phone call. On the other end of the line was a man who introduced himself as Capt. James Culp. He said he was a lawyer stationed in Seoul who worked for TDS. He explained that he was assigned to my case and that if I accepted him as my lawyer, even for an initial consultation that was in no way binding, he would come see me within a few days. He also mentioned to me that even though he was a captain now, he had once been an infantry sergeant just like me. When I heard that, I thought, "Okay, he knows my kind." "Come on in," I told him. "Let's talk." He finished by saying, "Do not speak to anyone besides your doctors, nurses, family, and the people from the Japanese government you have already been dealing with. And even with them, do not talk about your case before I get there. No one. Do you understand?" "Yes, sir," I told him. "I understand."

A few days later, he showed up in my hospital room. He's a big bear of a guy and wore a suit rather than a uniform. He later told me that he chose to wear a suit against his boss's advice because he wanted me to know that he represented me, not the U.S. Army. And he was right. It helped put me at ease. I think I would have been more uncomfortable if he had showed up in full uniform.

He introduced himself, and we made a little small talk. He asked me what he should call me. I told him something we used to say ages ago in the army: "You can call me anything you want, as long as you call me three times a day for chow and once a month to get paid." So with that, he started calling me Charlie. I had never been called Charlie before in my life. Growing up, I was always Robert. When I was a teenager, I was Super. In the army, I was Jenkins. In North Korea, the three other Americans took to calling me C.R., while the Koreans sometimes called me Min Hyung-chan. (They gave me this name when I started acting—they needed something to put on the credits—but in person, I refused to answer to it.) So, although I have gone by many names in my life, Charlie was a new one. But now, thanks to Capt. Culp, a lot of people, especially everyone I now know in the U.S. Army stationed in Japan, refer to me as "Charlie."

After that, Capt. Culp took out a notebook, pointed at the ceiling, and scribbled: "We don't know who could be listening, so I am going to write."

I wrote back, "OK."

He tore the page off and wrote, "Were you kidnapped?"

I wrote back, "No."

He wrote, "Did you decide to cross the DMZ on your own?"

I wrote, "Yes."

"Why?" he wrote.

For all of that session and for much of the time I spent in the hospital, we did a lot of our communicating silently, using hand-written notes.

Capt. Culp spent many full days with me those first few weeks, asking every little thing about my desertion and case. He told me everything I was accused of—desertion, aiding the enemy, soliciting others to desert, and encouraging disloyalty— and we talked about all of the things that I did and did not do. I was accused of a lot of stuff that I simply didn't do. Part of the "soliciting others to desert" and "encouraging disloyalty" charges, for example, were based on the prosecution's assertion that I had made propaganda broadcasts across the DMZ, during which I supposedly told American soldiers to turn their guns on their own officers and come join me in the North. But I never made any broadcasts across the DMZ of any kind, much less ones saying things like that. Dresnok, Abshier, or Parrish may have, I don't really know, but I never did. And then, some of the stuff that I did do, such as teaching English the first time, from 1973 to 1976, Culp successfully argued to prosecutors that I did out of fear of grievous bodily harm if I refused (which was true), and in a military court, that can often make you innocent of the charge. Eventually, Capt. Culp and I decided that I would plead guilt only to one count of desertion and one count of aiding the enemy (for my second stint teaching college English, from 1981 to 1984).

After a couple of weeks and many, many sessions, Capt. Culp went to Camp Zama, the U.S. Army base about an hour outside of Tokyo, to negotiate with the prosecutors who were going to try my case. He left in the morning and was back in the hospital by the afternoon. When he came back, I could not believe my ears: While Capt. Culp told me that the prosecution could not formally guarantee anything until I had actually turned myself in, he said that he had gotten a verbal commitment that they were willing to accept a pretrial agreement sentencing me to a maximum of thirty days in jail.

A lot of people who are in no position to know such things confidently declare that my jail sentence was some sort of political arrangement brokered at the highest levels of the Japanese and American governments. This could not be further from the truth. While both governments may have agreed diplomatically and informally that it would be in the best interest of both countries if there was an amicable solution to my case, and there may have been some conversations about me at the highest levels, the United States, all the way up to President George W. Bush, always maintained that my case would never be resolved without going through proper legal process. And today, I am grateful for the United States' hard line. Once the process was established, there was no outside manipulation or pressure put on the army about my case by anyone. I am grateful that the United States said no special deals would be cut on my behalf, since that allows me to say today that I have made my peace with the U.S. Army and have done the time it judged appropriate.

Obviously, my welfare was helped immeasurably by the Japanese government—it got me out of North Korea and to Japan safely—but in the end, even it had to step away from the American military justice system. The way I see it, the Japanese government got me all the way to the gates of Camp Zama, and for that I am forever grateful. But once I was there, I was on my own, with only Capt. Culp to help me. And after all was done, my legal fate was left to the prosecution, the defense, a judge, my commanding general, and no one else.

On September 11, a car came to pick me up at the hospital and
drove me to Camp Zama. There, in front of a pack of TV cameras and reporters, I got out of the car, walked up to Lt. Col. Paul
Nigara (the provost marshal of the U.S. Army in Japan), gave
him my best salute, and said, "Sir, I am Sgt. Charles Robert Jenkins, and I am reporting for duty." With that, I became, as far as
I know, the longest-missing deserter ever to return to the U.S.
Army. While awaiting trial, I was still an active-duty soldier, so
the army put me to work. That first day they issued me uniforms,
an ID, and a standard-issue sergeant's family quarters, which
was a nice, old, three-bedroom house on a shady hill on base. They
gave me a haircut and made me a member of the Headquarters
and Headquarters Company, United States Army Garrison,
Japan. My day-to-day job was to process new people who came
to the base. Led by company commander Capt. Dave Watson, all
of the people in Headquarters Company were very nice to me.
They made me feel at home beyond anything I could have expected. Not only did they teach me how to use the computer, and
the phones, and whatnot, they went out of their way to show me
that while I was accused of some very serious crimes, they were
able to separate the man from the deed. Everybody at Camp
Zama was also incredibly kind to my family, who were very
frightened and on unfamiliar ground and appreciated every bit
of the hospitality that was extended to them.

I could not believe how much the army had changed. The
most striking thing was the level of familiarity between officers
and enlisted men. In the 1960s, enlisted men and officers ate in
different mess halls and used different latrines. More than that,

however, if a soldier back then wanted to talk to an officer, he needed to get permission from his squad leader. These days, anybody can talk to anybody he wants. Back then, you got paid in cash. Now, your money is deposited in your bank account. After I reported for duty at Camp Zama, I opened the first bank account I ever had.

Although everybody at Camp Zama was as good to me and my family as I possibly could have asked for, I would not have gotten through this time without Capt. Culp. He quickly became the only person in the world besides my wife that I trusted 100 percent. As we worked on my case together in the hospital and during the month and a half I was at Camp Zama, I became convinced he was a very good lawyer. But he also became a very good friend of mine. Even though I had done a terrible thing as a soldier, it meant a lot to me that he did not judge me. Since he was stationed in Seoul, I know that being away from home for so long on my behalf was very hard on him and his wife and two small children, who got to see very little of him for nearly six months.

I think that is part of the reason he took so strongly to my family. Brinda, Mika, and my wife might not speak very much English, but they can understand it pretty well, and they appreciated his clowning around, trying to put everyone at ease. For example, one time when I was in the hospital, I had just gotten my blood pressure checked. My wife was about to leave so that Capt. Culp and I could begin more work on the case. She kissed me goodbye, and Capt. Culp called the nurse back in to retake my blood pressure to see if my wife's affection had gotten my blood racing. Sure enough, the blood pressure had gone up.

Brinda and Mika quickly became crazy about Capt. Culp, too. When we first went to Camp Zama, he was with us when the girls got their first look at the PX. Even though the PX at Zama is pretty typical by Japanese or American department store standards, this was one of the first real stores they had ever seen. In Pyongyang, even the best stores are mostly empty, dingy, and dusty. Here, the shelves were sparkling and filled, overflowing with food, clothing, electronics, and cosmetics. More things than they knew were available in the world were right there in front of them. They just about lost their minds. "Give them some money, Charlie," Capt. Culp demanded. I had not gotten the advance on my first month's sergeant pay yet, so the only money I had in the world was what was left of the $2,000 the high cadre had given me the day before I left for Indonesia. And I am tight anyway, so I was going to give them a few dollars apiece. But Capt. Culp was having none of that. "C'mon, Charlie!" he said. "Give them some real money!" So I looked at him and them and peeled off a $50 bill for each of them. No doubt, it was the most money they had ever held in their lives. They squealed, snatched the bills, and were off, almost running through the aisles, looking for things to buy. "Look at that," said Capt. Culp. "If the North Koreans knew that the money they had given you was undoing years of communist indoctrination in just a few minutes at a store on a U.S. Army base, I wonder what they would say?"

It wasn't all about money, of course, but once we arrived in Japan, I would say it took only a couple of days before both Brinda and Mika were fully convinced that leaving North Korea was the best decision we had ever made. Sometimes these days, as a joke, I will say to Mika, "Maybe we should go back to North Korea after all. What do you think?" And her response is immediate: "You have a good time while you're there, 'cause I ain't going."

Later, just before the court-martial, Capt. Culp had to go back to Seoul for a few days. Brinda and Mika became very upset when they heard the news. They were afraid that he wasn't coming back. In order to convince them, he left his dress green uniform in the front closet of my house at Camp Zama as proof that he would return. Brinda was actually going to shine his shoes for him while he was gone, but I stopped her, saying I had told Capt. Culp and he was touched, but he said they were already shiny enough.

Getting my dress green uniform together for the trial proved to be a task, since there are no infantry units in Camp Zama. I had to borrow an infantry braid from someone on post, and Capt. Culp had to get some of the ribbons for my left breast pocket in South Korea. Since I knew that my pretrial agreement limited my maximum confinement to thirty days, I was not as scared walking into that courtroom on November 3 as I would have been otherwise, but I was still mighty nervous. The proceedings took a whole day. Military court differs from civilian court. In civilian court, you can plead guilty to pretty much any crime you want, no questions asked. But in military court, if you plead guilty, you still go through a process, called a providence inquiry, where the judge has to decide whether you are really guilty of the crimes you say you are. Then, at the end of the procedure, the judge (or it can be a jury, it depends) issues a sentence. At that time, the punishment included with the pretrial agreement is opened and compared to the judge's sentence. The guilty soldier then gets the lesser of the two sentences. At the end of the day, after hearing me plead guilty to and explain my crimes, the judge sentenced me to six months in jail, but she also recommended to my commanding general, Maj. Gen. Elbert Perkins, that he throw out her sentence entirely for clemency's sake. (Capt. Culp later told me that my judge was the chief trial judge of the U.S. Army, and she had flown in especially to hear this case. Her recommendation to suspend my sentence out of clemency was only the second time in her career that she had done this.) My commanding general denied her request, so that meant my thirty-day pretrial jail sentence went into effect.

People talk about the "light" sentence that I received, but I think the people who matter—the judge, the lawyers, the commanding general of Camp Zama—understood what many people always seem to forget when they say I got off easy. Forty years is a long time to be a deserter and to live in an enemy country—if you are there by choice. While I walked to North Korea by choice—a crime I confessed to and fully regret—I did not stay by choice. I was forced to stay there. I am thankful that the people who truly controlled my fate understood that one crucial fact: I made a mistake by deserting, but once I had crossed the DMZ, I was trapped in a country that is little more than a giant prison.

That night, after having dinner with my family and my company commander, Capt. Watson, and 1st Sgt. Eugene Moses at my home on Camp Zama, a helicopter picked me up and took me to the brig at nearby Yokosuka Naval Base. I was released five days early, for good behavior.

10 | Homecomings

A few days after my release from jail, my wife, daughters, and I departed for what I hope will be the final stop in my life of strange travels: my wife's hometown of Mano on Sado Island.

For many years, when we were stuck in North Korea, Hitomi and I would ease our homesickness and loneliness by telling each other stories about our homes and families for hours on end. We would describe every little detail: the shops we went to, the places we hung out at with our friends, what we used to have for dinner. But as I listened to her tell of the high green mountains, the blue ocean waters, and the flat rice paddies of Sado, I never dreamed I would actually lay eyes on them. And now, not only was I here, but it was my new home, too. After an all-day journey, we arrived at the ferry port on December 8, 2004, to great fanfare and media attention. Hitomi had been living on Sado for the twenty-one months we were separated, of course, and even Brinda and Mika had visited while I was at Camp Zama and in the brig, so I was the only one of the family for whom the place was all new.

The island is as beautiful as my wife told me, and the people are just as friendly. I moved into the small, two-bedroom house on a quiet street that Hitomi had already been living in. One of the first things I did upon my arrival was go to the hospital and meet my father-in-law. He was very sick and was expected to die in a matter of months. Through a translator, I told him I was very happy to finally have the opportunity to meet him, and I said I was sorry I couldn't have asked him for his daughter's hand the proper way. He told me that Hitomi had told him a lot about me over the past year and three-quarters and that he approved of the marriage and was happy to have me as a son-in-law. Thereafter, Hitomi and I would visit every other day or so until he passed away in February.

Soon after arriving, I walked around our nearby streets with my wife and met all our neighbors. I also got to know the mayor of Sado very well. He has taken a special interest in our family and has done everything he can to make sure we are fitting in as well as possible. I was also introduced to Keigo Honma, although everyone calls him by his nickname, Kakuhon-san. He speaks excellent English and volunteered to be on call to help me whenever I needed to take care of routine things that can be unexpectedly difficult for a foreigner, such as opening a bank account, applying for a residency card, or going to the hospital. Since then, he has also become one of my best friends, and I don't know what I would do without him.

Once I had settled in, my wife and I turned our attention to our next biggest hurdle: traveling to the United States to see my mother and the rest of my family in North Carolina. Getting the trip underway took a bit longer than I expected. First, there was some paperwork to take care of with the army. Then, my father-in-law died, and my wife and I decided it was important to observe the traditional mourning period of forty-nine days. At the same time, however, my father-in-law's death only emphasized to us how fleeting life is and how urgent it was to rush to the United States while my mother, who is ninety-one years old, was still alive.

Then there was the matter of my passport. While I had made my peace with the U.S. Army justice system, the U.S. State Department, which decides who gets a passport, still needed to be satisfied that I had not committed any "expatriating acts" or anything that would make me ineligible for a passport. Usually, things like becoming the citizen of an enemy country, serving in the military of a foreign country, or working for the government of a foreign country are reasons enough to throw an American's citizenship and passport eligibility into doubt. Since I had already publicly declared in my court-martial that I had both been a North Korean citizen and government employee while teaching English (although almost every job in North Korea is a government job), the embassy told me that I had to come in for a face-to-face meeting.

I was very worried that I was not going to be given a passport, but the man at the embassy in Tokyo explained to me that the State Department's rule of thumb was "to look more at intentions than actions." He explained that if I did the things I did because I feared for the safety and well-being of myself and my family, and if I never actually desired to relinquish my U.S. citizenship, then I was probably still in good standing with the U.S. government. That's when I knew I would be okay on this front: No matter what I did in North Korea, I never, ever intended to renounce my U.S. citizenship. The man at the embassy then gave me a written affidavit to fill out, asking me for more details about my history, which took a few hours.

While we were waiting for the passport to come through, I also had to figure out how we were going to fund the trip. I am well aware that there are many people in Japan who resent everything that the Japanese government has done for me. (Some even begrudge the assistance the government has provided to my wife.) And I know that there are some who see me as a freeloader. That is why it has always been very important for me to find a long-term means of support for myself and my family. I have no intention of being a burden on the Japanese people. That is part of the reason it was essential to me to fund 100 percent of this trip out of my own pocket. Fortunately, the contract for the Japanese edition of this book was coming together at the same time as I was planning for the trip, so I was able to bring my daughters and wife to the United States to meet their family without Japanese taxpayers' money.

On June 14, my family and I left Tokyo to achieve a dream that over most of the last forty years I never thought would come to pass: We were headed back to my hometown. My sister Pat and brother-in-law Lee picked us up at the airport and took us to their large, beautiful brick home right in the heart of historic Weldon, a town not far from Rich Square, where I grew up. As we entered the house for the first time, my mother was there waiting for me. I just cannot put into words the feelings that came over me as I laid eyes on her and gave her a hug and a kiss. It was a moment that I will never forget.

Pat had warned me ahead of time that our mother's Alzheimer's had become very advanced over the past year. Our reunion was dramatic and emotional, but I have to admit that it probably meant more to me than it did to her. She knew I was her son Robert and that I had been gone a very long time, but there was not much more that she was able to comprehend. As with many people suffering from Alzheimer's, she had good days and bad days. Some days she would be able to recognize and register who Hitomi and I were. On other days, she would confuse me with my brother, Gene, or really not even be able to make out that we were her children at all. There were times that it was very sad to watch, to see this woman who had always been so strong and such a powerful figure in my life laid low by her failing mind.

I try to live my life without regret, and no part of my journey out of North Korea could have been helped or speeded along, but I do wonder what it would have been like to be reunited with my mother when she still understood everything and I could have explained to her everything that had happened. I am so happy that I got to see her, and that she was still coherent enough when I got out of North Korea in July of 2004 that she could at least understand that I was not a communist defector who lived there by choice or abandoned his family on purpose. But I am sorry and sad that she had slipped so far into Alzheimer's by the time I arrived that I could not tell her all the details myself.

My trip home was, as much as possible, a private affair spent catching up with all of my long-lost relatives and friends. All of my surviving siblings came over to Pat's house at various points throughout the week. Some of my old buddies from Rich Square came over one evening. And many nieces and nephews visited as well, some flying in all the way from California to see me. We just sat in Pat's living room talking about the old times, and I told stories about what life was like in North Korea. Everybody was excited to meet Mika, Brinda, and Hitomi. I doubt my daughters

ever realized they had such a large family. I am extremely grateful to have a family like that, one that was supportive of me all
the years I was gone and continues to be supportive now. A big
highlight of the trip was also filling up on all the Southern home
cooking I had been missing for decades. Smoked ham, black-
eyed peas, macaroni and cheese, cornbread, seven-layer salad,
and pineapple upside-down cake—and that was just one meal.
My daughters developed a particular fondness for the cornbread
Pat would make.

We did try to get out of the house as much as we could, but the
Japanese media, who were camped outside Pat's house and followed us wherever we went, made that very difficult. It is hard
to overestimate just how famous my wife is in Japan and how
much media interest there is in her every move. For our trip to
the United States, every Japanese network, newspaper, and wire
sent a full crew to report, multiple times a day, on the details of
our visit. They followed us wherever we went. I understand that
the media just had a job to do, and I am thankful that people
seem genuinely interested in our story, but I wish we could have
had more time to ourselves. We visited my father's grave and
drove around some of my old haunts in Rich Square. We went
shopping a few times, went bowling, and had dinner or lunch at
restaurants a couple of times. One day we took a trip to the North
Carolina Zoo, which Brinda and Mika particularly enjoyed.

I was amazed at how much the area I had grown up in had
changed. Since I had managed to stay somewhat current with the
outside world while I was in North Korea by listening to the
radio or watching smuggled videotapes, my culture shock in either Japan or America was not as great as you might expect. I had
never used a computer before arriving in Japan and had never

seen one in real life, for example, but thanks to the movies, I knew what they were, what they did, and what they looked like. But the size of things in America did surprise me. We went to a Wal-Mart, and even compared to Japanese stores, the place was enormous. Same with cars. Japan makes some of the best cars in the world, but the cars in the United States (even the Japanese-made ones) are so much bigger than the cars in Japan. The other big surprise I had in the United States was how completely integrated society was and how equally whites and blacks treated each other. It was clear that the South had made a lot of progress in that regard over forty years.

I was a little surprised, to be honest, at what a controversial figure I was in my hometown. I knew that I was infamous, and that my status as a suspected defector and my appearance in North Korean movies had made it very difficult for my family, but since I had been out for a while and thought that the accurate details of my story were fairly well-known, I did not expect the more extreme and hate-filled things some of my critics in the United States said about me. More than what they said, I was surprised at why they said it—that is, I was surprised at how ignorant people were about my case and what North Korea is really like. Going AWOL to avoid combat is a serious crime, and abandoning troops under your command is one of the worst things a military man can do. I know that, I have admitted that, I am sorry for that, and I have spent my life having to live with my conscience and the consequence of my actions on that day; at my court-martial, I asked the U.S. Army's and America's forgiveness. But clearly that message had not gotten through back home. Maybe it is partly my fault—perhaps I have not been vocal enough about my regret—but upon my arrival in America, I was astonished to learn that some people were convinced that I was a communist sympathizer and willing defector, that I had spent forty years in North Korea by choice ("I don't know why he chose to come out now if he liked it there so much," I heard one lady interviewed on the TV news say), or that I did things like appearing in movies or teaching English to military cadets because I wanted to.

I sometimes wonder if my critics know just how common a military crime desertion is and how rare lengthy jail sentences for it really are. I do not imagine everyone will be able to forgive me for what I did, but all I ask is that those who judge me at least know what they are judging me for before they say things like I should be lined up against a wall and shot. That said, I did receive a tremendous amount of support and goodwill from the vast majority of people I encountered and heard from while I was in North Carolina. I think it is significant that the only strangers who approached me on the street were those with a kind word and a smile, a pat on the back, and a "Welcome home."

Upon returning from the States, I focused my attention on finishing this book, which was published in Japan in October 2005. When that was done, I turned my attention to removing one of the biggest obstacles standing in the way of living a happy life in Japan: not having a driver's license. Since no driving schools on Sado or even the largest nearby mainland city of Niigata had English-speaking instructors, I moved to a small boarding house just outside of Tokyo and enrolled in the Koyama Driving School.

Everyone there was very nice to me, but getting my license was not easy. I went for lectures and driving lessons every day. I was a great driver in the United States and in the army: When I was stationed in Germany, I was even in charge of the motor pool. But I had not driven a car in forty years, so I was pretty rusty. And with all of the signs in Japanese, many of the rules of the road so different than those in the United States, and driving on the left side of the road, I had my work cut out for me. I would go home every night and read the books and try to memorize all the rules for driving. But since I was never much for book learning, this was pretty slow going. And the days when we drove on real Tokyo streets made me so nervous, I never got any sleep the night before. Psychologically, it was very tough. But with hard work and lots of dedication, I made it. And I am glad I did, because now I am more confident than ever. One of my instructors told me, "If you can drive in Tokyo, you can drive anywhere," and I believe that is true. After twenty days of lessons, I went back to Niigata, and on my third try, I passed the driving test.

When I returned to Sado, I bought a Daihatsu Move, and I cannot tell you how happy being able to go where I want, when I want, has made me. Later, in the spring of 2006, I even went back to the same Tokyo driving school to get my motorcycle license. In Japan, you don't need a special license to drive a 50cc motorcycle, so for a while I would tool around Sado on that. But it is so small and slow that you need to ride on the shoulder of the road with all the cars whizzing past you. To me, that felt pretty unsafe, so I went back to driving school to get a proper motorcycle license. Since I knew all the basics, getting my motorcycle license took me only ten days. Now, on nice days, I will ride around Sado on a 250cc Honda Magna that I bought. That is a lot more power than a 50cc, but it is still a lot easier to manage than the bikes at the driving school, where instructors make you learn on a 400cc.

After all of the commotion surrounding the book's initial publication, my life has finally settled down to a very comfortable routine. Every morning, my wife and I get up and have coffee and breakfast together. Between 8:00 and 9:00, Hitomi leaves for her job at city hall on Sado. Most days around that time, at least during the summer, I head out to my farm. Well, I call it my "farm," but at 225 by 100 feet, it is really just a big garden on the land attached to my father-in-law's old home. Every year I plant corn, tomatoes, peppers, cucumbers, cabbage, watermelon—a whole bunch of stuff. I plant so much that it is more than Hitomi and I can eat, and we wind up giving a lot away to neighbors or a local restaurant we like to go to. I also tend to the rabbits my wife and I keep.

After I check on the garden for a little while, I head out to work. I work seven days a week. On weekends, I work at the Sado Gold Mine, which is one of Sado's major tourist attractions. I am a groundskeeper there. On all other days, I work at a cookie factory at Rekishi-densetsu-kan Park in Mano City. That park is also a big tourist attraction, and the cookies from Sado are famous and one of a kind. I work in the store, helping to stock the shelves and meet the guests who come in. The people of Sado have gotten used to having me and Hitomi around. They don't even glance twice when they see us on the street and around town. But tourists who come to Sado from other parts of Japan, they are a different story. When they see me in that shop, they just about go crazy. (Their reaction when they see Hitomi, if they happen to catch her out on the street, is even more extreme.) I shake their hands, pose for pictures, and speak to them as well as I can, considering how bad my Japanese still is. That is one of the parts of living in Japan I am most sheepish about: My Japanese still isn't very good. The manager of the cookie factory is happy to have me, because my presence makes a lasting impression on the guests and maybe gives them one more thing to talk about at home when they return from their trip to Sado. Recently, in fact, the cookie factory started putting a sticker with my name and signature on it on every box of cookies. My wife was against that at first. She thought it was too much, me acting like my head was too big, like I was some sort of big shot. But I told her I didn't think anyone who gets up every morning and farms and works in a cookie store could really have too big of a head, and after a while she agreed that that was probably true.

During the evenings, my wife and I usually enjoy a quiet dinner at home and watch TV or a movie. Every Monday, I help out with a local English class, just to give the students more practice speaking with a native speaker. Sometimes my wife and I will go to dinner with some of my wife's coworkers at one of a number of small restaurants on the island and finish up with karaoke at a nearby bar. I am particularly fond of singing Elvis Presley songs. (Former prime minister Koizumi is also an Elvis fan.) On weekends, I often go fishing with a coworker from my wife's office. The fishing on Sado is excellent: I frequently bag fifty fish in a day. If my daughters are in town for the weekend, the whole family will take a day trip to the beach or go hiking. I haven't really gotten the hang of our home computer, except to check the news and print photographs, but I think I would have an easier time if the operating system wasn't in Japanese. Lately, I have taken up photography, and I like to shoot home movies with my video camera.

To be honest, I do not have many big hopes or plans for the future. After living for forty years in North Korea, just to be out and living in freedom and comfort in Japan with my wife and daughters is more than I ever thought I would get out of life. If I do have hopes for the future, they are modest ones. My biggest desire is that my wife and I continue to have a good life at home together on Sado and that my daughters make the most of their futures, building lives that make them happy and fulfilled. It is up to them to determine what will make them happiest, of course, but I imagine that would mean a husband, children, good jobs, close friends, and a lifetime of good health.

My daughters live in Niigata with a family originally from Sado as they go to college. After months of studying only Japanese, they passed their Japanese fluency exam in April 2006, and now they are taking courses that more directly focus on their careers. Mika has decided to be a kindergarten teacher, so she is enrolled in a local teachers' college. Brinda, meanwhile, wants to go into the wedding and events planning business, so she is currently studying at business school. They come home for a weekend once a month or so, and I am always so happy to see them. I am amazed at how quickly they are growing and how well they are adjusting to Japan. But their futures are now up to them, and I thank God that they are in a place where they are able to make such choices. Our choices are what make us who we are. Nobody knows that better than me.

Text : 11/15 Granjon
Display : Granjon
Compositor : Binghamton Valley Composition
Printer and Binder: Maple-Vail Manufacturing Group